MW00675381

DR. DONALD ARNETTE

I AM

SUPPOSED TO BE HERE

The Art of Dealing with Perception

SPIRIT REIGN
PUBLISHING
A Division of Spirit Reign Communications

Author: Dr. Donald Arnette
Cover Design: Daryl S. Anderson, Sr.
Page Layout & Design: OA.Blueprints, LLC
Editor: Springhawk Publications, LLC

© 2015 Dr. Donald Arnette. All rights reserved.This book may not be used or reproduced in any way without the expressed written consent or prior permission from the copyright holder. Reprinting the content as a whole or for giveaway or resale is expressly prohibited.

Printed in the United States of America.

ISBN's:
978-1-940002-66-8 (HB)
978-1-940002-67-5 (ePDF)
978-1-940002-68-2 (ePUB)

SPIRIT REIGN
PUBLISHING
A Division of Spirit Reign Communications

ACKNOWLEDGEMENTS

I'd like to take this opportunity to thank the people that have been instrumental in my success. None of this would have been possible without Dr. Melanie Cobb. She motivated me, supported me, had unwavering confidence in me, and inspired me to be the best I could be and maximize my potential. Words can't express how much of an impact she's had on my life and my career.

I want to express my gratitude to my entire family. My parents laid the foundation, which allowed me to know the value of hard work and to always do things the right way. To my wife, Kim, who has been my rock and never stopped believing in me. and my kids Daylin, Dylan, and Danielle who are my inspiration.

I'm also very grateful to the countless friends who have given me support through this process. I'd also like to thank Ruthie and Lori for writing support.

PREFACE

I've had many opportunities to speak to a variety of audiences throughout the country, consisting mostly of young people. Whether it's at a church youth group or career days at various schools or other settings, one of the things I endeavor to drive home, especially to inner-city kids, is that we as a people need to redefine what success looks like.

There's a pervasive mindset among young people today which suggests that the historical portrait of success is a middle-aged Caucasian male, wrapped in an Armani suit, wearing a pair of wingtip shoes and carrying a briefcase. It's a sad commentary, to say the least, but that seems to be the agreed upon traditional representation of a successful individual.

Each time I speak to a group of young people, regardless of the venue, I request that the coordinator not reveal my educational background, my Doctorate degree or anything else relative to what I do for a living. I want everyone to realize success can look just like them. When I speak to these kids, I typically dress down in jeans, t-shirt and tennis shoes. What I also like to do is offer $20 to anyone who can guess my occupation. Sadly, I've never had to hand over that $20. In classic stereotypical fashion, they assume I'm a rapper, an athlete, model, and once I was even labeled a construction worker. It's interesting that on opposite ends of the spectrum, and often by completely diverse groups, I can be judged by my outward appearance.

It's painfully clear that we need to change how minority young people view success and themselves. We need to dramatically alter their distorted perception of what heights they can reach, so they don't solely aspire to be a rapper or believe that athletics is the ultimate achievement and representation of success.

I want to go on record as saying there are many phenomenal athletes who have done great things for our communities and continue to do great things for our communities as well as inspire young people to be the best they can be. This is not to take anything away from them and their success. The point I'm making is that young minorities should never place a cap or limitation on their capabilities and what they can accomplish. They shouldn't seal themselves up in a box labeled "Rapper" or "Athlete" only.

I've encountered many speed-bumps on my road to success, which you'll read about as you turn the pages. The important thing, however, is that I have not allowed my speed-bump to become a road-block. We'll all face challenges in one way or another. Yours may be similar to mine or completely different, but, in any event, the key is to persevere, be committed and realize the term "minority" is a statistical reference that does not, and should not, define what I or anyone else can become or what level of success each of us can achieve. If we can eradicate the image of the hip-hop/rap-star role model that has been deeply etched into the minds of our young people, it's possible that someday the age of stereotypical judging could cease to exist.

I want to state very clearly that this book is not about racial profiling or racism. It's about knowing who you are, taking responsibility and realizing what it takes to be successful. It's about working hard, being dedicated and knowing how to react appropriately when you're met with negative perception.

I also want to make it clear that this book is not a "woe is me" monologue or an invitation to my "pity party", nor is it a "soapbox" speech. It's a book about overcoming obstacles, leaping every hurdle that stands in your way, staying the course and not allowing circumstances to become hindrances.

Life is like a chess game - not checkers;

It's a marathon, not a sprint.

[The authorship of these quotes has not been researched]

CONTENTS

1

THE EARLY YEARS

I would say, technically, I was a middle child. I have two older sisters and a younger brother. I'm sure most of us have heard several different definitions and/or opinions about the middle-child-syndrome. A Stanford University study suggested that middle children were most envious, least bold and the least talkative. Other studies say middle children are trailblazers, willing to compromise and excellent negotiators. I don't know if I fit the widely-accepted profile of the average middle child, but I was definitely always different. When you're the firstborn you have an instant identity as the oldest. Likewise, when you're the last born sibling you're identified as the baby. Those of us who are children in the middle can attest to the fact that we often create our own identity and individuality apart from that of our siblings.

My siblings and I were fortunate to be raised in a two-parent household where, early on, my father and mother instilled strong values and work ethic into us. Growing up, I was no stranger to hard work. I remember my brother and I, essentially, had the same responsibilities and routine chores to perform around the house. We got up every morning to feed the horses, and *Oh* how we hated weed-pulling duty. The day-to-day toil and drudgery was something I suppose most kids our ages loathed then and still loathe today. But those tiresome chores were character-builders that taught me responsibility and laid the groundwork for my life. I learned the value of hard work and the importance of following through and finishing what you start.

My brother is two and a half years younger than me and we were always very close, although we did have our moments of sibling rivalry. He loved basketball as much as I did and those backyard battles became a regular occurrence. He was always trying to beat me to prove he was the better athlete. But, of course, I could never let that happen because having my younger brother out-play me would have been quite a blow to my psyche back then. One time during one of our games we got into an argument that turned into a fight. My father was down working in his garden and saw us scuffling. He ran up and scolded both of us for fighting with each other. He reminded us that, as brothers, we should never fight one another because we have a duty to take care of each other. On occasions my father would come outside and watch us play ball, which was pretty cool. We especially loved it when dad would referee because it gave my brother and me a chance to show off and dazzle dad with our astounding hooping skills. We each always tried to outshine the other. I would say sibling rivalry most often reared its ugly head when we played basketball.

Eventually, my brother did become a better basketball player than me, and went on to play professionally. While I'm obviously very proud of him, I can't help but think that all those one-on-one backyard competitions helped prime him for the pros.

One of my sisters was a bit of a rebel, so to speak. She seemed to have an eye for the boys at a relatively young age. My brother and I didn't interfere or try to hover over her the way perhaps older brothers would have. Maybe we could have tried to be more protective but she was older than us so we pretty much stood back and let her make mistakes. Back then, we thought it was funny and not really that big of a deal. We were young and had very little written in the pages of our lives at the time. I would later learn that, given the right circumstances, a rebel-spirit can be advantageous in some instances. Going against the grain when the grain is going the wrong way can sometimes be an asset rather than a liability.

At about age nine, my father asked us kids how we wanted to live when we grew up. I told my dad I wanted a better life than his and my siblings'. Moreover, I wanted to be rich. So, my dad said the only way I could fulfill my desire for wealth was to become a doctor. That was a problem because my passion was basketball. Being an athlete was the only thing on my radar at that time. I wanted to follow in the footsteps of my idol, Julius "Dr. J." Erving. When my father asked us that question we were too young to realize it then, but he was planting a seed that in time would take root and blossom. Dad was a great role model for us. He grew up in Mississippi and eventually worked his way up the ranks from a typist to a senior executive for the federal government. He became a top-level executive without a college degree. He's a prime example of what hard work and dedication can do. It's never too early to start planting those seeds and challenging your kids to think about what they want out of life and what path they want to take.

In fourth grade, I attended a private school and played on my first basketball team. I was ecstatic, although it was short-lived. Knowing how obsessed I was with the sport, my father said I was focusing way too much on basketball and not enough on academics, so he withdrew me from that school. In retrospect, I can't help but wonder if there might have been another reason he took me out. Granted, I was fanatical about basketball but I think the main reason could have been that my parents simply couldn't afford to send all three of their children to private school, and that's not something you can easily convey to a child. So, off to public school I went. It was four years before I played on another basketball team. Even though my heart's desire was to play pro ball, I didn't have blinders on. I had a backup plan in the event things didn't pan out. I decided Science was going to be my alternative field. As a kid, I didn't immediately get on board with the whole doctor thing. That career path was recommended by my parents because of my intellectual ability and desire to be wealthy, but it was not my first choice.

In my early academic life, junior high and high school, the problems I encountered in school were not a result of behavioral issues or insolence on my part. The problems were primarily a result of me being somewhat academically advanced. I imagine there aren't very many people who would consider excessive intelligence a problem, but it sometimes became an issue for me because it threw me out of sync with my peers and classmates. I wasn't a perfect kid—there's really no such thing. I went through the turbulent teens just like my peers did, and I also did foolish things that got me into trouble. I remember one night just before my seventeenth birthday, my brother and I decided we'd go bowling. We picked up a few other friends and we all hung out and had a good time. It was about 10:30-11:00 p.m., and we all should have just gone home but we weren't ready to call it a night yet. So, there we were — five bored teenage boys cruising around town; nothing about that recipe spelled disaster, right? Wrong! One friend had the brilliant idea that playing mailbox baseball would bring some excitement to an otherwise boring night. I was completely against the idea at first. I felt uneasy about it because I knew it was wrong, and because I knew it was just a bad idea. But, wanting to fit in and not be the killjoy in the group, I went ahead and agreed to do it because everybody else was on board with it. So we got some baseball bats and the night's festivities began. I was driving a pickup truck inches away from the curb while my friends (the batters) were in the back of the truck whaling away at mailboxes on the road. These were nice mailboxes too, because it was an upscale neighborhood. At that time, we were clueless about the ultimate damage we were doing; we were just foolish kids thinking it was fun. Then we pulled up to a really attractive mailbox and just as my friend did his backswing getting ready to smash it, we saw a car driving up toward the house. I'll never forget that car, it was a mustang convertible. Evidently, it was the couple who lived in the house with the fancy mailbox. The man was driving and he pulled up and stopped to let his wife out as we sped away. She went inside (as we later found out) to call the police and he drove off after us. There we were with an angry homeowner hot on our trail. I could see the mustang in the rearview mirror so I knew he was still chasing us. I had to obey traffic laws so I had no choice but to slow down and/or stop at one point and when I did, all my friends and my brother jumped out of the truck and seemed to scatter in all different directions. I didn't know what else to do except keep driving. So I did. I was on my own and, unfortunately, for me, I was in an unfamiliar town so I had no idea where I was. Then like most teenagers, I had a brilliant idea! In the movies when one car is chasing another at night, the car being chased will turn off the road and shut their headlights off so they can't be seen. Hey, it always works in the movies so why wouldn't it work for me? I quickly turned off onto a side road and shut my lights off. I just knew my plan would work. What I hadn't planned on was blowing out my front tire when I made my great off-road escape. So, obviously, I needed to change the tire. I got out, got the jack and started jacking up the truck to change the tire. Moments later, a police car pulled up and the officer asked me what I was doing there. He asked what I had been up to that night and how I ended up there. I told him some people were chasing me and I was trying to get away from them. He asked if I was involved in the mailbox baseball caper; these were the police officers responding to the wife's call about us bashing in their mailbox. So he already knew I was involved because I'm sure the homeowner gave a detailed description of my vehicle. So there was no point in me denying it. I came clean and admitted I was involved, and was arrested and taken to jail. During the process at the jail, the officer looked at my driver's license and said, *"You're still a minor, you're not seventeen yet, so you'll have to call your parents to come get you."* It was 1:30 in the morning when I called home. That was the worse call I ever made. My dad answered the phone and when I told him where I was, there was a long pause that seemed like an hour.

Needless to say, it was a long ride home. My brother had walked back to our friend's house so he was safe and sound. I consider myself very fortunate to have gotten off with a citation. Actually, they were supposed to mail the citation to me but they never did. The officer also said that if any homeowners filed complaints against us we'd have to pay for the damages. Amazingly, no one ever did. My parents were pretty upset, and rightfully so. But, thankfully, I wasn't grounded for life. My dad is the kind of person who can't stay angry for very long. He gets over things pretty quickly; like the time when I was about twelve and my brother and I tried to ride our bikes down the stairs in our house... the "L-shaped" stairs. We were sure our little Evel Knievel stunt would work, why wouldn't it? But as you might expect, it didn't. We went sailing into the wall and knocked a gigantic hole in it. We were grounded for a while but in classic dad style, he always had mercy on us. He ended up putting a vent there and moving on. His inability to stay angry is one of the many wonderful qualities he has and I'm grateful that I took after him in that regard because I'm the same way with my kids. I can't stay angry with them either. Yes, I did my share of crazy youthful antics but I never went too far.

***

I was a gifted student, an over-achiever and always had lofty goals and ambition but I never wanted this to be known by my peers. I never disliked school, in fact, my initial high school experience was great until we moved, and I had to go to a different high school that was predominantly white. Changing schools is always tough for kids. Nobody likes being the new kid on the block and trying to find a spot in the social circle of the school. It can be especially difficult when you feel ethnically out of place. The kids at the new school were nice enough—many of them attempted to befriend me, but I still felt like an outsider. I'd get invited to various parties and other social activities, but I never really felt like a part of the group. There was one other

African American student there named, Nathaniel Quincy, who became my best friend. We were both basketball enthusiasts and were the best players on our team. One day, during one of our games, Nate collapsed on the court and the game was stopped. He was taken to the hospital where he was pronounced dead. It was a devastating tragedy that left me distraught. After Nate's death, I really was alone at school and it was the worst kind of loneliness. It was a terrible blow losing my best friend, especially while we were playing a sport we both loved. That kind of trauma was hard to deal with. I walked around in a fog the rest of the year. I hadn't known that kind of grief before and it pretty much consumed me. It was a while before I was able to fully function again.

In ninth grade, my mom gave me Dr. Ben Carson's book, *Gifted Hands*, along with his later book, *Think Big*. Reading those books ignited a desire in me to be like Dr. Carson—a world famous neurosurgeon. He talked about all the obstacles he faced on his way to becoming one of, if not, the most notable neurosurgeon of his time. He was an inner-city kid raised by a single mother, which some might say put him at a distinct disadvantage in life. But he rose above his circumstances and prevailed over the streets that could have led to his failure and demise. When I read Dr. Carson's books, little did I know that much like him I, too, would face challenges and have giants to slay on my journey to success.

2

ON TO COLLEGE

When it came to college, I was under the misguided impression that because of affirmative action, being a minority was more or less a rite of passage, which meant I didn't have to overly apply myself to gain acceptance. I thought the *powers-that-be* would rally around me because I was an African American male pursuing higher education. I couldn't have been more wrong. It was that same mindset that led many young minority students down a bumpy road in their pursuit of professional degrees. Generally speaking, I'd say my grades were very good but not exceptional—they were far beneath my capability. Looking back, in my opinion, affirmative action did more harm than good to *some* minorities, because it fostered a belief that being black and a little above average was enough to get you through. That mentality brought about an academic complacency that was counterproductive and not at all conducive to real learning. In high school, we had been told by former students that it was okay to perform poorly your first two years of college because the institutions didn't expect you to do that well the first couple of years anyway. That was a bunch of bull! It doesn't matter whether you're a freshman, sophomore, junior, whatever—you should always do your best. The focus should be on actual learning and not just getting by. In retrospect, I regret that I foolishly believed I didn't need to put my best foot forward or strive for excellence because I had been told I could glide through on the wings of affirmative action. There have been times I wished I had never heard of affirmative action because I allowed it to obstruct my pursuit of academic excellence. The *guaranteed acceptance* concept of affirmative action led me to do just enough to get by, even though that idea was contrary to my nature, my upbringing and everything I believe in.

I graduated from college the same year the Hopwood

vs. State of Texas decision eliminated affirmative action from Texas schools. It was a lengthy case but after the initial court's ruling, race was no longer the basis for admission to institutions of higher learning. Therefore, I had to continue my education without the benefit of presumed preferential treatment. At its core, affirmative action was a crucial step in the right direction because there were, indeed, inequities that made it very difficult for minorities to get equal chances at education and employment. However, what I didn't like was the resultant mentality of *some* minorities who only viewed it as a free ride.

I still had my sights set on becoming wealthy but my grades weren't as good as they should have been. They were acceptable but they didn't represent my true capabilities. My athletic career aspirations fizzled out after chasing my basketball dream from the University of Texas at Arlington, to playing at a junior college and ultimately ending in West Virginia. A knee injury made it imperative for me to decide what career-path I would take. I had to get serious about my future.

Since I had graduated from the University of North Texas with a degree in Biology, for all intents and purposes, it should have been time to mosey on to medical school, right? Not quite. Instead, I decided the better plan would be to apply for a job at the local medical school and network with some of the well-connected people on the "inside" who could guide me through the admission process and help me get into medical school with less hassle.

When I went for the job interview, I met with Dr. Melanie Cobb, a woman who really changed my life. She had already seen a substantial number of other candidates and by the time I interviewed with her she had pretty much already decided on the person she would hire. She only interviewed me as a courtesy because I was scheduled to come in that day. Not knowing that she had already made up her mind to hire someone else, I went in all set to impress her and do and say everything possible to get the job. Surprisingly, my spiel worked! And I was hired. Initially, I didn't think much of the job, probably because it was too easy for me—it just didn't challenge me. As time passed, Dr. Cobb began to notice my borderline apathy and indifference toward the job, so she started trying to convince me to apply to graduate school. At that particular time, graduate school wasn't something to which I had given much thought. I figured I still had time to kick other things around. However, after an encounter with a very rude student, I decided to give graduate school some serious consideration. I don't know what his problem was that day but he did a pretty good job of ruffling my feathers. Apparently, I hadn't cleaned my area the previous night to his specifications. So, he proceeded to yell and curse at me while I was standing in the hall talking with a friend. I refused to stoop to his level of insolence, so I didn't yell back. I didn't say anything to him. It wasn't because I was afraid or intimidated—I would have had no problem fighting and pulverizing him right there on the spot. But believe it or not, at that moment, I actually took the time to think about the consequences that would follow if I responded with violence. I thought about how I'd be placing my future in jeopardy because of this one incident. So, I simply walked away. I was seething because I felt powerless and trapped by the circumstances. I'm sure there was commentary among those who witnessed it, but I'll never forget those last venomous words he said to me, *"Just do your stupid little job."* I'm sure he said that in an obvious attempt to belittle me because he thought he was better than me. That's when I decided to let him and everyone else know I was just as capable as they were. I wanted to show everyone who might have looked down on me that I could do anything they could do; I could achieve as much as they achieved, and more. So, I applied to graduate school.

I was sure I would be a shoo-in since I had worked for one of the most prominent researchers on campus for a year and a half, and she was the one who encouraged me to apply. So I thought my acceptance was pretty much a sure thing. But, my well-executed, well-thought-out plan didn't quite go the way I expected. It wasn't solely a matter of my grades and test scores because they were good enough for admission. The issue, as communicated to me, was that I didn't appear to be dedicated enough, and that was a field that required dedication and commitment. Consequently, as a result of my dedication being in question, they came up with an alternative plan designed to "please everyone". The solution was to admit me as a special student, which meant I was not officially in the UT Southwestern program but I was taking classes on, more or less, a trial basis. If my performance for one semester was satisfactory, then I would become a regular student like everyone else in the program. I found the whole concept a little puzzling, inasmuch as the outcome was predicated upon me showing that I was dedicated enough to join my peers as a regular student. That *special student status* was bizarre, at best. In my opinion, it wasn't an ideal litmus test to gauge my future dedication. I'm sure many students have gone into programs with a great deal of dedication only to find themselves losing interest halfway through. I'd even venture to say we all know someone who has changed their major or been on the verge of rethinking their whole academic career at one point or another. So, I seriously wondered how they would be able to give an accurate assessment of my dedication to a four-to-six year program after only one semester. How could they possibly think that four months was ample time to evaluate my dedication? Looking back, I now realize they were in a win-win situation regardless of the outcome. If I succeeded they could safely say, "We knew you could do it that's why we gave you a chance." On the other hand, if I had not succeeded they could have safely said, "We really didn't think you could do it anyway that's why we didn't give you regular admission." Either way, they were sittin' pretty in the driver's seat. Neither my success nor my failure in the program would have had any adverse effect on them whatsoever. To be honest, the whole thing was pretty insulting but what could I do? It was during that time that I realized I couldn't make decisions based on hyper-emotions or pride. Sometimes you just have to "play the game." So, graduate school, here I come!

3

GRADUATE SCHOOL

Graduate school was a unique experience unlike anything I had ever experienced before. My fellow-students were mostly Asians and Caucasians whose main focus was school. They were academic marvels; intellectually gifted—extremely smart. There was one other African American guy in my class who was pretty cool but he didn't last beyond the first semester. I was somewhat disheartened that he didn't or perhaps couldn't see it through for whatever reason, but after he was gone I, once again, felt like the odd man out. I was well-received by my classmates; I think they were intrigued with me because in all probability I might have been the first African American man they ever personally interacted with. Oftentimes, I have found that, we let fear of a cultural clash prevent us from getting to know people who don't look like us. It's as much a cultural impediment as it is a racial one. Instead of dealing with people on an individual one-on-one basis and getting to know exactly who they are, we spend far too much time categorizing and grouping them collectively into the box society says they belong in. I'd venture to say if we stopped classifying people based upon how they look, we just might find some genuinely good people with similar hopes, dreams and desires for their lives.

When it came to academic excellence, I was definitely among the "cream of the crop" and I refused to give credence to the myth that African American students were inferior and less capable than Caucasian or Asian students. This was going to be the first time I truly challenged myself and I could really feel the pressure. But what continually drove and motivated me more than anything else was I didn't want to let Dr. Cobb down after she had gone to bat for me. She was the one who told me I had what it took to be successful as long as I persevered. She had more confidence in me than I had in myself. So there was a lot at stake.

I was pretty nervous in the beginning because I was at one of the best graduate schools in the nation and the material was, initially, over my head. I was thoroughly confused the first couple of weeks but after a short while I figured it out. I was determined not to give anybody the satisfaction of seeing me fail. In addition to that, I wanted to succeed for my own sake. It wasn't just that I wanted to show other people I could do it, I wanted to prove it to myself also. So, I put my nose to the grindstone and committed myself to doing everything I needed to do to excel.

I'll never forget the day I was strolling around the lounge looking at pictures of the alumni for that program. I noticed two glaring consistencies; each year the class size increased, and there were no black men shown in any of the pictures. My curiosity got the better of me so I asked around to see if any other minorities, specifically black students, had completed that particular program. To my surprise, the answer was a resounding—no! I was shocked but also excited because it meant that if and when I graduated I would be the first black male student to complete it.

That was an astounding realization. I hadn't initially set out to become any kind of forerunner or pioneer, I was just seeking a higher education. I had no idea I would end up, essentially, making history. It's a classic example of how life can put you in places you never thought you'd be.

I did extremely well on our first test, which earned me an unexpected trip to the Dean's office. I was puzzled, maybe even a little nervous as to why he wanted to see me. I remember thinking to myself, '*he couldn't suspect me of cheating because that would have been virtually impossible with that particular test.*' Of course anything was possible and for all I knew someone could have accused me of cheating or something. So with a small amount of trepidation, I went to the Dean's office. Thankfully, it turned out he just wanted to tell me that I had done a good job and to keep up the good work. Then he added, "We knew you could do it, that's why we gave you a chance." He said those famous last words I had thought about earlier. I didn't find it the least bit flattering as some people might have. I was actually a little offended by the patronizing,

borderline belittling attitude that accompanied his statement. I thought about how they initially questioned my
dedication when, in reality, they just didn't think I had the
aptitude to succeed at that level.

While enduring my *special student* status, I'd have regular
visits with the Dean where he would recite the usual – "*everyone was proud of me*" speech, and tell me to keep up
the good work for the rest of the semester. It made me feel
like a less-than-capable, intellectually-challenged charity
case. I didn't like the condescending overtones but what
could I do? Quit? Not a chance. So, I just kept smiling
and saying, 'thank you for the opportunity.' As I said earlier, sometimes you just have to play the game. Did acqui-
escing make me any less of a man? Absolutely not. That
university had something I wanted, which was a doctoral
degree, and I was willing to do whatever it took to get it. I
had to tuck my ego away and continue my pursuit.

I was hopeful that my *special student* status would only
last through the first semester, but that hope was thrashed
because the second semester was just like the first, but I

weathered it. Then finally the day came when I had my last visit with the dean. He congratulated me for successfully completing the first year of graduate school, and informed me that I no longer had special student status. At last, I could join the ranks of my regular classmates without wearing the scarlet letter label of "*special student*." Every doubt they had about my dedication and commitment miraculously vanished in just eight short months. It was a huge relief when the *experimental* phase was over, then I could focus on finishing my education in a normal fashion.

Graduate school is somewhat unique in terms of what you'd normally expect of a school regimen. For one thing, you only have regular scheduled classes for about the first two years. Year two, you only spend about thirty-percent of your time doing actual class-work. The majority of a graduate student's time is spent doing complex research projects that are primarily the determining factors for when you will graduate. To some degree, you can set your own schedule in graduate school within reason of course, and you have a lot of flexibility. So it's not at all uncommon for students to work on projects at staggering hours. I had a classmate who worked fourteen hours a day, six days a week, and then worked another eight hours on the seventh day. He was a prime example of how there's no such thing as a normal schedule for graduate students.

I was blessed with the ability to perform research and get things done in a timely manner, which I was really happy about because those skills became very useful as I went through school. I could do in six hours what it took my classmates ten hours to do. This was somewhat of a blessing and a curse. I remember at the end of one of my rotations, Dr. Thomas wrote my evaluation which was positive overall but he included the following statement: "Don is extremely bright but he exudes a cavalierness that may be perceived as a lack of dedication or commitment". This was my first introduction to the potential power of perception. Even though I was extremely thankful that everything I undertook pretty much flowed seamlessly I had to be careful to make sure it "looked" like I was working hard. I just knew I was on my way to realizing the success I had dreamed of most of my life. I had worked hard to get where I was. I was zealous and enthusiastic about where I was going in life. You might say I was sure there was nothing but blue skies, green pastures and good fortune ahead for me. I had no idea that just ahead, in my immediate future, was something that would forever change my life.

4

AN UNEXPECTED EVENT

It wasn't unusual to study or do certain research projects on the weekend, in fact, it was pretty common. It was around four o'clock that Sunday afternoon in October of 2002, when I headed to school to get some work done. I got out of my car completely oblivious as to what was about to happen to me. As I was walking across the courtyard, a police car drove in and parked. There was nothing out of the ordinary about a police car driving into the courtyard, so I didn't think much about it and continued on my way. As I was heading toward my building, the officer got out of his car and approached me. The first words out of his mouth were, "Where is your I.D.?" I was baffled as to why he came directly to me when there were several other people in the courtyard. I asked him why he was asking for my I.D. to which he replied, "Because you don't look like you're supposed to be here." I was on my cell phone at the time and I looked at him and said, 'What did you say?' He had no problem whatsoever repeating himself and again he said, "You don't look like you're supposed to be here." Then he added, "Look at you." By that time, I was basically speechless—in total disbelief. I was still on my cell phone with a classmate and I asked her if she heard what the officer said to me. She, in fact, did hear the whole thing and said, "Wow, that's messed up." The officer then instructed me to hang up my phone. Again, I asked him why I was being singled out when there were so many other people around. His initial explanation was that everyone else had come from the visitor's parking lot, which didn't make any sense to me because that's where I had come from. It quickly became apparent to me that the only reason I had been singled out was because the officer saw a black man on a prestigious university campus. He went on to say he thought I looked suspicious because I was wearing sweats, which was preposterous since the school's workout facility was right beside the building I was walking toward. I could very well have been going to work out. That fact alone underscored how ridiculous it was for him to say my sweats caused him to detain me. Nevertheless, this officer was holding firm to his assertion that I looked suspicious because of my sweats. While he was giving me the third degree, another guy walked by who was also wearing sweats. I saw that as a golden opportunity for me to make it known to this officer that I wasn't naïve as to what was really going on there. I knew the whole episode was racially motivated. The other guy wearing sweats was white, and I shouted to him, "Hey, you need to come over here and speak with this officer because you are wearing sweats and that, in and of itself, is suspicious." The young man turned and started walking towards us but the officer motioned for him not to come over. So I said to the officer, "Wait a minute, you said this was about my sweats." He completely ignored what I said and didn't respond to my comment. At that point, I knew for the first time in my life I had come face-to-face with hardcore racism. I had never experienced it up close and personal before. As an African American, I knew the history of racism; I've read the books, seen the movies, and heard stories passed down from my ancestors, so I'm aware of its existence. But I wasn't raised to be prejudiced against any ethnicity. Racism, bigotry, intolerance, etc., those things were never taught in our home. Furthermore, while we're all aware that racism is still out there, living in the 21st century, I never expected to be in the center of such a brazen exhibition on a college campus.

I had told the officer my name at least three times and still he repeatedly asked, "What's your name? Why are you here?" It would have been very easy for him to verify my affiliation with the university but instead of confirming the fact that I was a student, he chose to call for backup. Everything was happening so fast. Before I knew it, eight more officers had arrived and surrounded me. I was flabbergasted, I hadn't done anything wrong and yet the officers that had just arrived were saying things like, "Let's not make this go from bad to worse." And just like the officer who initially detained me, another one shouted, "What are you doing here?" Others took out their pepper spray, and some just stood there watching. Quite honestly, at that point, I must admit I was afraid for my safety. I was in the middle of a wide-awake nightmare and I didn't know how I was going to get out of it unscathed. At that moment, I realized just how quickly a person's life can change. In a matter of minutes my day had gone from being just another ordinary day to me being surrounded by aggressive officers who were giving me the third degree just because I was a black man walking on the university campus with sweats on.

Thankfully, the lead officer on the scene finally got the others calmed down. Meanwhile, I was still baffled as to what I had done wrong. Then the lead officer asked what my name was. I was growing increasingly frustrated with telling them my name over and over. I told the lead officer I had given my name several times already but he said, "You need to tell me." So I obliged him and said, "Don

Arnette." By then, I was a bundle of nerves. A barrage of emotions just flooded over me all at once. I was angry, I was hurt, I was humiliated, I was embarrassed, I was scared, but I couldn't change anything that was happening. I was completely powerless and it was a horrible feeling. I vocalized to the lead officer how outrageous and completely uncalled for the whole thing was but he had no response. Seemed like it was no big deal to them at all. To be fair, I know that police officers deal with a lot on a daily basis, but you would think that the supervising officer would have at least made a simple phone call to verify that I was a student, but he didn't. I was trapped; standing there for what seemed like forever. I didn't think the situation would ever end.

As the insanity continued, I saw a Caucasian woman walking toward me and the horde of police officers. It was Dr. Margaret Phillips. I was well acquainted with Dr. Phillips because her office and lab were right next door to my mentor's office and lab. I remember thinking, *thank God Dr. Phillips just walked up*. I said to the officer, "Look,

here's one of my professors, she can tell you who I am."
As she got closer to us she looked at one of the officers
and said, "What are you doing? That's Don Arnette, he's
a student and a good guy." Another officer asked to see
her I.D. She complied. At that point, I thought the whole
thing was about to be over because my identity had been
verified by one of the faculty members. But no such luck.
After examining Dr. Phillips' I.D., the officer told her she
needed to leave the area, and she was escorted away from
the chaos. Meanwhile, I'm standing there fuming. Finally
I said, "I'm leaving, my professor has told you who I am."
The officer fired back with, "You aren't going anywhere."
I said, "Why not?" He said, "You are officially detained." I
said, "For what?" His response was unbelievable. He said,
"Don't worry about it."

Don't worry about it? What kind of answer is don't worry
about it? How could I not worry about being detained for
reasons that were completely unknown to me? I hadn't
broken any laws. I hadn't done anything except get out of
my car and start walking across campus. Yet I was being

detained. I didn't know what to do. I felt trapped like a tiny fly in a giant spider web. I was livid and in utter disbelief.

I'm painfully aware that many young black men are *stereotypically* viewed as thugs, mainly because of their outward appearance and the way they carry themselves. But I was a graduate student at one of the most prominent, highly-respected institutions in the country. I didn't look the part, I didn't look like a gang member nor did I walk or talk or act like a thug. Nevertheless, none of that mattered because at the end of the day, I was still black. When you think about it, that's a very painful reality. You really don't have to do anything wrong. Just walking along minding your own business can still result in you being detained by law enforcement. Even so, you have to keep your cool.

About twenty minutes after the "Don't worry about it" comment, the officer looked at me and said, "All right, you can go." I couldn't believe the madness was actually coming to an end. At first I didn't think he was serious, I thought at any moment he was going to change his mind and further detain me. After a few seconds of hesitancy on my part, I started to walk away. However, to my dismay, I wasn't walking alone. Believe it or not, the officer who initially detained me escorted me into the building and stood beside me as I was waiting for the elevator. I had an uneasy sinking feeling in the pit of my stomach as we stood there. Why on earth did he think I needed a police escort to the elevator and then to my destination? It just didn't feel right. So, when the elevator arrived, my commonsense and survival instinct took over, and I looked at him and said, "I know you don't think I'm gonna ride in this elevator alone with you." He looked at me and said, "Why not?" I said, "You just had your pepper spray all set for me. Plus I had to ask your fellow-officers to take their hands off their revolvers. And now you think I'm gonna get on an elevator alone with you? I don't think so."

There's no telling what he had in store for me once we were alone in that elevator. He obviously thought I was ignorant to the ways of the world, but he was mistaken. He didn't say anything else after that he just looked at me with a devious smirk and walked away.

I've told several friends about the events of that day and many of them tell me different ways they would have handled the situation and what they would have done. But until you've been in that kind of predicament, you have no idea how you will react. It took every ounce of self-control I could muster to stay calm and not lash out. I had every right to be infuriated and would have been justified in blowing my top and going on a tirade. But that would have just made matters worse, and warranted whatever their reactions ended up being. If I had lost my temper I would have given justification to them for what they were doing to me.

As an African American male, you have to be mindful of what to do and what not to do when you have an encounter with a police officer. You cannot "give them a reason", you must keep your cool and be cooperative and submissive. That is not a blow to your manhood; on the contrary, it's simply being wise and knowing how to survive. That's just the way things are. It's a harsh reality, but it's reality nonetheless.

Sadly, African American males are often portrayed as perpetrators of violent crime, so it's almost expected of you to act violently. But I wasn't falling into that pit. It's heartbreaking because I believe many young minority males resort to a life of crime because they feel it's expected of them anyway, and when they don't see any hope for a brighter future they just give in and assimilate right into the stereotype. Young minorities need to realize that the challenges and obstacles they face trying to educate themselves and succeed in life pale in comparison to the toll a life of crime takes on you. If you're going to struggle and claw your way through tooth and nail anyway, why not let it be for something that elevates and lifts you up rather than something that tears you down? Put all that effort and energy into educating yourself so you can rise above the low-level expectations of society.

As you might expect, that incident with the campus police didn't just dissipate, it stayed with me. I was so upset about it I couldn't stop rewinding and playing it over and over again in my mind. While it was happening I couldn't do anything because I was in a precarious situation. At that moment, I had no choice but to comply and back off but that didn't mean I was going to back down. While I was on my knees surrounded by all those policemen, I felt like I had been transported back in time to the civil rights movement when men such as Martin Luther King, Jr., Medgar Evers, Malcolm X, and other civil rights leaders were on the frontlines fighting for equality. It was then that their cause became very real to me, and I finally understood with unmistakable clarity what they had been standing _against_ and what they were fighting _for_.

I should mention that prior to the whole police incident, I met a wonderful woman at the University of Texas at Arlington who became my wife. I had seen her around for quite some time but never had enough courage to talk to her until I saw her at a party. We hit it off immediately and were married several years later. We had a simple courthouse ceremony because I was what you might call the proverbial starving student at that time and couldn't afford a lavish wedding. We subsequently had three beautiful children, Daylin, Dylan, and Danielle, and I didn't realize that the aftermath of what I went through with the police incident would seep into my family and gradually start to affect the peace and harmony in our home. I didn't know it had traumatized me the way it did. But over time it started to trickle into my family and other areas of my life. The subsequent events stemming from that incident with the police put an enormous amount of pressure and stress on our family. And the aftereffect was by no means over.

5

HOW DO I RESPOND?

Human nature causes you to want some kind of vindication or retribution when you've been wronged. But there's a right way and a wrong way to respond to injustice. I knew I couldn't just toddle along as though nothing had happened; as if my life was just as it had always been. It wasn't. My life had changed dramatically. I wasn't nursing a bruised ego or driven by a need to get some kind of revenge. It was a simple case of wanting to be treated with the same courtesy and consideration that I showed to others. And that's not an unreasonable expectation. What fueled my desire to take some sort of action was the need for justice.

I spoke to my mother about the incident shortly after it happened and she suggested I file a complaint with the Office of Equal Opportunity. I decided to take her advice and the next morning I went to file the complaint.

There may be some people out there who would say I should have just let it go and forgotten about it. Some might go so far as to say I was overreacting or making too much of it. But I suspect the people who would say those things have never experienced that kind of public humiliation and violation of their basic human rights. Believe me, I wasn't whining or being unreasonable—that's not the kind of person I am. I was standing up and making it known that I was a human being with the same God-given rights that every human being has. No one should think they have the right to demean another human being because of the color of their skin or for any other reason. I realize there are times when it isn't just about skin color; people are demeaned for many different reasons these days. We've seen stories in the news far too many times about kids committing suicide because they're being bullied mercilessly. Sometimes it's classism; people are degraded and looked down on because of where they live or how they dress or the kind of car they drive. Kids in the inner-city are thought to be beneath those who live in the suburbs. And it doesn't end there. So, I knew with this incident I couldn't just look the other way. It wasn't all about me and my rights, it was also about smoothing out the road for our kids and future generations to come.

When I filed my complaint with the Office of Equal Opportunity, I was pleased when I discovered an African American man was going to be in charge of the investigation. I figured he would be impartial and fair. The process itself was going to be different because I was a student filing a complaint rather than an employee. Typically, that office handled complaints filed by workers. So I understood that procedurally it was going to be a unique process. I sat with him and answered questions as he made notes and remarked how terrible and inappropriate the officers' actions were, and he assured me that he would aggressively investigate the incident. I felt at ease because I sensed his zeal to make sure the officers were held accountable.

After my meeting with the investigator, I headed back to the lab. I saw Dr. Phillips on the way back and she looked at me with compassion in her eyes and said, "You look like you need a hug." She told me how sorry she was that I had gone through that experience and she described the officers involved as a pack of wild dogs. I appreciated her support and was really touched by her empathy and concern. It was nice to know she didn't condone the way they treated me. I hadn't yet told Dr. Cobb about the incident or about filing a complaint and I felt that I should be the one to tell her about everything that was going on. I didn't know what to expect as far as how she would react to me filing a complaint. She was an important member of the faculty and when I filed the complaint, for all intents and purposes, it appeared to be against the school even though my grievance was with the campus police. So I was a little concerned about what her reaction might be. When I told her about the incident she was devastated; so distraught over the events that she cried. However, she didn't seem overly optimistic when I told her about the complaint I filed. The vibe I got from her suggested she may have thought it bordered on being a waste of time. Nevertheless, I was hopeful for a favorable and satisfactory outcome.

About three days later, I received a phone call from the investigator informing me that he had completed his investigation. I felt mildly vindicated and was glad I had taken a stand; my voice had been heard and I was ready to move on with my life. I was pretty excited on the way to his office because I was fairly confident that when I got there the results would be in my favor. I was wrong. He cordially invited me into his office and engaged in a bit of small talk before handing me a stack of documents. As I sat there reading through them, it became almost as arduous as the encounter with the university police. In essence, the documents stated that the investigator found absolutely no fault on the part of the officers in question. The investigator had read the officers' incident report and spoke with them. The officers portrayed me as belligerent, aggressive, and uncooperative. This was like pouring salt in my wounds. Not only had they wronged me but they wanted it to appear as though the whole thing was my fault. I was depicted as the stereotypical angry black man. He did, however, see the need to make certain recommendations that would prevent misperceptions of racial profiling in the future. And that was supposed to make me feel better? Solve everything? Make it all go away? By recommending that steps be taken to prevent any chance of misperceived racial profiling was essentially implying that I mistakenly felt racially profiled—it was all just a misunderstanding on my part, according to him. The crux of these cutting-edge recommendations would include sensitivity training for university police, and a campus-wide policy requiring all staff and students to display their university-issued I.D. badges at all times. I was not pleased with that outcome, in fact, it made me angry. I wasn't asking for anything earth-shattering, just an acknowledgement that I was an innocent person whose civil and basic human rights had been violated.

After that huge letdown, I wondered what I was going to do next. I could have just walked away and forgot it but something inside of me needed a more satisfactory conclusion. I had been treated unjustly and I wanted justice.

The sensitivity training and new campus policies were all well and good, but it was like putting a tiny Band-Aid on a gunshot wound.

I did a little research and discovered I could appeal the investigator's decision to the Vice President of Human Resources, so that's what I did. Oddly, I still had a pre-conceived belief in the justice system. I was considerably naïve. When I met with the Human Resources V.P., things seemed to go well. She, too, was African American. During our meeting she asked me for a dollar figure to present to the administration—this was before she had done any investigating on her own. She said it would make things easier if they had a sum in mind. I hadn't said anything about any sum of money; the subject of financial compensation hadn't come up at all until she mentioned it. So, that led me to believe it was going to be a pretty quick, open and shut case. Once again, I was wrong. She said she'd get back to me in a few days after she had done her own investigation of the incident. I didn't give her a dollar amount—I couldn't because for me it wasn't about money. Despite popular opinion and worldview, not everything can be solved with money. You can't put a dollar amount on the worth and value of a human being.

The next several days seemed like an eternity while I waited for her call. Then, four days after our initial meeting she called and asked me to come to her office. I told her if she was planning to give me a letter similar to the one the first investigator had given me, she could mail it. She said she needed me to come to her office, so I went. To my surprise, she had a video of a significant portion of the incident that had been captured by one of the officer's dashboard cameras. She and I watched the video and at the end she asked, "What did you see?" I said, "I saw a man being harassed by confrontational, unprofessional officers." She agreed with me, and slid a document across her desk to me. In the document, the officers were described as unprofessional and it also acknowledged that they exhibited behavior that was totally inappropriate. I thought, *'Good! Finally I get some kind of satisfaction.'* However, as I continued to read, I found that I had been depicted as an angry, belligerent young black man. It went on to outline the same recommended sensitivity training and mandatory badge-wearing that the first investigation letter contained. With that, the process was concluded and no further action would be taken by the university. And that was it. The system failed me and no one in a position of authority with the power to help me seemed to care. It was like nobody wanted to rock the boat; let's just turn a deaf ear and look away. I felt like I had been kicked in the gut. I told her she wasted my time and that she could have mailed the letter to me for all the good it did. It hadn't solved anything.

I went home and tried to figure out what my next move would be. I wasn't going to let it go because I knew I wanted to make a difference not only for myself but for other minorities and future generations of every ethnicity.

When I entered college/grad school/medical school, my goal was to get an education and make a nice life for my family and myself. I had no idea I'd be setting precedents and finding myself in the center of a racial dispute. But before I knew it the whole situation had taken on a life of its own. As I said earlier, I realized that in the big scheme of things this was not just about me anymore. There's an age-old quote that says something to the effect of: *All that's necessary for evil [wrongdoing of any kind] to triumph is for good men to do nothing.* There comes a time when you have to do something—take a stand for what's right. But in doing so, be very mindful of the way you approach any kind of adverse situation. You should always address conflicts and adversarial issues the right way. Not by violence or disorder, not by viciousness, deceit or cheating. You have to keep your wits about you and make <u>justice</u> your goal not <u>revenge.</u>

6

A STEP FURTHER
- LITIGATION

After both investigations failed to produce any kind of satisfactory results, I started considering other options. Many
of my buddies are professional athletes, and one in particular happened to have an agent who was also an attorney
that I had gotten to know pretty well. So, I consulted with
him about my ordeal and shared the chain of events with
him. At that point, I didn't see any other recourse or reme-
dy for me except a lawsuit. During the consultation, it was
clear the attorney was hesitant to take on such a landmark
case. He explained that it would be a tough road to travel
because suing the university, in essence, meant suing the
state of Texas, and that would be a huge undertaking for

any attorney. He had misgivings about taking the case for a number of other reasons; one being he had just opened his firm and didn't feel he had the resources or wherewithal to litigate a huge case like that. I understood his position perfectly but I was still determined to see it through, which meant I had to find an attorney who was willing to take the case. I decided to do it the old-fashioned way. I took out the phone book and just started calling one attorney after the other. I don't know how many I spoke to before I found one who agreed to take my case. At the outset, he cautioned me that since I was still a student at the university, things could get difficult for me on campus. I told him I could handle it. I was already weathering the front end of the storm, so a little more rain wouldn't make much difference. I was all in. My attorney filed a civil rights violation on my behalf against UT Southwestern Medical Center and the grueling process was on. When the higher-ups at the university found out about the lawsuit, they were indignant. They said, "How could you do that to us? We're the people who gave you a chance." While that was true, it didn't really have any bearing on the issue at the forefront of the case. I appreciated the opportunity they had given me but, opportunity notwithstanding, my civil rights had been violated in a most embarrassing and humiliating way. I had been put on display and treated like a criminal simply because of the color of my skin, and that was wrong. My position was very clear; I wasn't going to let it go.

The Dean called me to his office one day and asked if I wanted to transfer to a different school. He was nice about it and said under the circumstances he would understand if I wanted to. I told him I appreciated his concern but I wasn't going anywhere, I was going to finish what I started. I was slated to be the first African American male to graduate from that program and I wasn't about to tuck-tail and run away.

From the time the case was filed to the giving of depositions was approximately a year and a half. By the time the depositions began, I was three years into my education at UT Southwestern. I knew it would be a difficult process but I didn't know it was going to be quite as involved as it became. As the plaintiff, I had to fact-check every individual's deposition, which meant I had to read each one in its entirety. And there were quite a few. All the police officers gave depositions; Dr. Phillips and Dr. Cobb gave their depositions; my classmate, whom I had been on the phone with that day, had to give a deposition and, obviously, I had to give mine. As I read through them, one was particularly hurtful because I realized the person I believed was genuinely in my corner wasn't as on-my-side as I initially thought. I had been portrayed in an entirely different light—described as agitated and unruly. There might have been a time during the ordeal with the campus police officers that I became visibly (and justifiably) frustrated, but I was not unruly or combative in any way. Still, there it was... in the deposition. I didn't understand why one of my biggest supporters had seemingly forsaken me and changed the original account of what happened. I can only surmise that there must have been reasons for the sudden change—reasons that I was not privy to. But life is too short to hold grudges so I moved on and have no hard feelings about it.

As you might expect, tensions were running pretty high at school but I had to stay on track. Even with the lawsuit going on, I still had to focus on my education because that was my ultimate goal.

More often than not, the wheels of justice don't seem to turn very fast. It seemed like the initial process and preliminary proceedings were taking forever. As we got closer to a summary judgment, each side was hoping the judge would rule in their favor. The summary judgment was basically the court's decision as to whether the case had enough merit to proceed or whether it would be thrown out. Naturally, the opposing side was hoping to get it thrown out while my attorney and I were hoping we'd be able to move forward with it. We waited on pins and needles for the judge's decision. I was hopeful but I knew I had to also remain realistic because it could have gone either way. And in light of the fact that every odd seemed to be against me, I didn't allow myself to be overly optimistic about anything. Then came the day when we got word that the judge had ruled that the case could proceed. That, in and of itself, was quite a victory for our side.

It was a tough time for everyone. Having a family and being a full time student was difficult enough, but then when you factor in the stress of suing the institution of which you're a part, the pressure is indescribable. Not only was it stressful for me it was also very stressful for my family, and even for the administration at school. It had become such a source of angst and tension that one of the powers-that-be called me into his office one day and said, "This thing needs to go away. How much will it take for you to drop this lawsuit?" He offered me a sum of money to drop the lawsuit but I told him I couldn't accept it. I had gone too far to turn back. Plus, the amount he offered me wasn't even enough to cover my legal fees. He wasn't pleased with my decision to proceed with the case, in fact, he was quite upset. He made me feel as though I was somehow harming him personally by continuing the lawsuit. It wasn't my intention to hurt anyone and I fully understood that the litigation affected many people at the university besides me. But the fact remained that it was something that needed to be done and I had to do it. If no one ever took a stand nothing would ever change. So the process continued.

7

HERE WE GO AGAIN

As I said earlier, the wheels of justice sometimes turn very slowly. Fast-forward to year four; the case is still ongoing. I didn't change schools I continued my studies at UT and graduation was just two weeks away. Campus life was nowhere near easy for me, especially during the lawsuit. Every place I went on campus I felt as though all eyes were on me. It was a horrible feeling to walk around under a perpetual spotlight knowing that I was being slandered—probably on a daily basis. But I persevered... I had to. I had gone too far to turn around. I had given almost four years of my life to that cause and I was determined to stick with it. You can start a million things but they don't mean much and won't make any impact unless you finish them. You have to dig deep and keep going no matter how many dirty looks you get. Even when you don't think you have the strength, if you look a little deeper inside yourself you'll realize it was there all the time, and you can draw from it when you're motivated by something that matters.

Even though I was winding up my academic career with graduation just two short weeks away, I wasn't off the radar yet. One afternoon when a colleague and I were coming back from lunch we saw a police car following us as we walked across the campus. My buddy remarked that we were being followed and I jokingly said, "You hang with me you always get a police escort." We just laughed it off and kept going. The patrol car had pulled up and stopped just ahead of us in the direction we were walking which meant we had to walk past it to get where we were going. I noticed the officer staring at us as we got closer to him and, in retrospect, I should have just kept walking and kept my mouth closed but I didn't. At that time, it annoyed me that he was leering at me like I was a criminal when all I was doing was walking with my friend across campus. So, I let impulsiveness get the better of me and I said, "Is there a problem?" He said, "No, I don't have a problem, you need to get your black ass on." I didn't say anything else to him, we just kept walking. Hindsight is always 20/20, and I see now that saying *anything* to him was the wrong thing to do. I should have known that nothing good would come from me asking a provoking question like that. And it didn't. Suddenly, I found myself at the threshold of what would be round two. The officer walked up behind us and asked for my I.D. After he examined my school I.D., he then asked for my driver's license—just mine. At no time did he ask my friend for any type of identification. It was interesting how, once again, he zeroed in on just me and not my friend who was white. My buddy and I both had gotten out of the same car and were walking together, yet, I was the focus of the officer's attention. I didn't understand why he wanted to see my driver's license because I was walking not driving. Plus, I had already provided him with my student I.D., so he could clearly see I belonged there. But be that as it may, he called for backup, reminiscent of the first incident. Here we go again. It was like an instant replay; déjà vu. Dr. Cobb was Dean of the graduate school by then, and I called her while we were standing there and told her it was happening all over again. She asked to speak to the officer. I held my phone out and told him the dean wanted to speak to him. He took the phone and hung it up. Meanwhile, like clockwork, other officers soon arrived on the scene. My buddy said to one of the officers, "Hey, do you know who this guy is?" The officer said, "No, who is he?" My buddy said, "That's Don Arnette." The officer replied, "The guy with the civil rights case?" My buddy said, "Yes." Then that officer got in his car and drove away. When I think about it now it's kind of funny that he just took off like that, but nothing was funny at the time.

Just like before, a supervisor/lead officer arrived on the scene. He asked the first officer what the problem was and he responded with, "This guy doesn't want to identify himself." I was astonished that he said that. I said, "What do you mean I won't identify myself? You have my student I.D.!" But, apparently since I hadn't given him my driver's license also it constituted failure to identify myself. That second encounter was just as unbelievable as the first. I was a university student walking on the university campus and proved my right to be there by providing my student I.D., but it wasn't enough. So the supervisor said, "Fine, then you're under arrest for failure to identify yourself." And they were dead serious. I was so stunned you could have knocked me over with a feather. I was handcuffed, they put me in the back of the patrol car, and I was taken to the UT Southwestern jail. Shocked doesn't even begin to describe how I felt. I was mortified. It was such an embarrassing and demeaning experience to be arrested and carted off to jail right there on campus in clear view of faculty, students, visitors and anyone else who happened to be within visual range. Having my colleagues and peers see me being handcuffed and arrested was beyond humiliating. My buddy, who had been walking with me just prior to the whole thing, went to tell the Dean what happened in hopes that she could pull some strings and expedite my release. Meanwhile, I arrived at the jail thinking how silly the whole episode was. I assumed they were just trying to shake me up or make some kind of example of me by arresting me rather than just giving me a citation for failing to identify myself. I figured at the jail they'd give me my ticket or whatever other formality they would go through and then I'd be on my way. Once again, I was wrong. They took my wallet and other belongings I had with me at the time, then they locked me in a room where I was handcuffed to a small bench. I sat there for almost an hour before anyone came in to talk to me. Then the officer came in and said, "Are you aware that you have a seatbelt violation you haven't taken care of?" I told him I didn't have any seatbelt violations. The whole thing was absurd. I reiterated that I had no such violation and that there had to be some kind of mistake. I was floored when he responded with, "Well, we'll just let you figure all that out down at the county jail." So they unlatched me from the little bench, slapped a different set of handcuffs on me and then transported me down to the county jail. It was beyond my wildest imagination; it just blew me away that I was actually being hauled down to county jail for an "alleged" seatbelt ticket I knew nothing about.

So, once again, I was put in the back of the patrol car and taken downtown. I was livid because it was so ridiculous. I couldn't help but voice my frustrations to the officer driving. I said something to the effect of, "Okay fine, take me to jail, but you're going to be in trouble for arresting me while there's an ongoing lawsuit." He fired back with, "You ain't nothin' but a uppity nigger." How does one respond to that? I was speechless. The first word that came to my mind was, Wow! I had no response. We all know that word is used more often than it should be in society. Unfortunately, in the African American community it's tossed around like some kind of term of endearment, and it really shouldn't be because there's nothing endearing about it. It's a derogatory term steeped in hatred and intended to reduce the African American to something less than a human being. I'd venture to say if young black people truly understood the denigrating history of the N-word, they wouldn't toss it around like a Frisbee. Nevertheless, in 2004, I never thought someone of another race, let alone a law enforcement officer, would say it to my face in such a demoralizing and vicious manner. I didn't engage in any kind of heated exchange with him. I didn't say anything else I just filed it away.

We arrived at the Dallas County jail. I want to state for the record that I didn't live the life of a saint. When I was a teenager/young adult I went to jail for some petty stuff like unpaid tickets and once I got into trouble with some credit cards, but I never committed any truly serious crime. What made this arrest so particularly devastating was that I was innocent; I hadn't done anything wrong. A decade or so earlier, I deserved to be there because I had, in fact, done what I was accused of—I hadn't paid the traffic tickets. But not this time. In addition to the obvious misfortune of me sitting unjustly in jail, I happened to arrive there the same week Dallas County was changing their computer system. The timing couldn't possibly have been worse. Basically, just like everyone else in there, I was trapped and couldn't get out because the new computer program wasn't even showing that I was in there. There was nothing I or any of the detainees could do. As the days went by, the jail was getting more and more crowded because more people were coming in, yet no one was being released. It was horrible. Jail conditions aren't good anyway but when you add overcrowding, tempers running high and horrible food to the already deplorable conditions, it becomes a dreadful and depressing place. The food was awful—a cinnamon roll for breakfast, a bologna sandwich for lunch and another bologna sandwich for dinner, none of which I was able to eat. Some of the inmates earned in-house titles because of their good behavior. Those inmates were known as trustees and they would sell generic brand Oreo cookies for fifty-cents each to the people in the holding tank. That was kind of the culinary highlight of the day considering how bad the food was.

After spending what seemed like forever in the holding tank, they finally called my name. I breathed a sigh of relief because I thought I was being released. But I was sadly mistaken because I wasn't being released at all, it was quite the contrary. I was taken to another room with about thirty or so other men and was told to put all my belongings, including clothing, in a mesh bag. Then, we were all told to shower. After the shower, we were given a pair of slippers, boxers and a white jumper inscribed with the words, *Dallas County*. The whole experience was beyond humiliating, I felt like I was in a herd of branded cattle. That's when the situation became real to me. I was terrified. Down through your life you often think you're pretty tough, but then you find yourself in a situation like that and you realize you're not as tough and infallible as you thought you were. At that point, you truly recognize your vulnerability, and it's a sobering reality. After I was all suited up in the jumpsuit that labeled me property of Dallas County, I was taken to a cell that I shared with two Hispanic men. In there, I was even more terrified because I was obviously outnumbered. In all the prison-type movies I've seen, typically, blacks and Hispanics don't get along too well in jail so I was expecting the worst. Fortunately for me, I spoke Spanish so we could communicate and they were actually okay guys. They even showed me how to adjust and regulate the temperature in the cell using, of all things, wet toilet tissue. Some of the guys in there were okay and just as frustrated as I was. But there were also inmates in there who were, shall we say, habitual lawbreakers and repeat offenders. I couldn't believe I was in there for some silly failure to identify and bogus seatbelt violation. I was in the company of some pretty hardcore inmates and feared for my safety on more than one occasion. What made it particularly frustrating was that I had no idea when I would be released. It was one of the worst times in my life.

I went through a range of emotions that are almost indescribable. I'll admit that, initially, I was a little smug during the second encounter with the police officer because I had my I.D., and foolishly thought there was nothing else they could do to me because of the first incident. I thought once they found out who I was they'd release me and apologize all over the place. Then after they arrested me every ounce of my arrogance and assuredness turned into anger and confusion. And then after that officer hurled his racial dart at me it added insult to injury, and I went from being angry and confused to being insulted and hurt. I was in an emotional typhoon being tossed all over the place with no safe port to hide in. And to top it all off I was sitting in jail for doing absolutely nothing wrong. There were times I was almost reduced to tears. Being innocent of any crime and helpless to change the situation is a feeling you can't adequately describe.

Finally, I got in touch with my attorney and told him what was going on. He seemed oddly pleased when I gave him a rundown of what happened. He said, "This is great! Do you know how much this helps our case?" At that moment, I couldn't possibly have cared less about the case, I just wanted to get out of there!

So, when I was finally being released, as part of the release process they give you paperwork that has your name, date of birth, case number, offense and other judicial jargon. On the way out, I was given my paperwork that contained or should have contained all the particulars of my case. As I was reading through it, I noticed that they had described me as a white male born sometime around the 1950s with a last name similar to mine but it was spelled Arnet. Suddenly, it became clear to me what was really going on beneath the surface. Then, a chilling portrait of spite and malice began to materialize. It was crystal clear to me that not only had I sat in jail on a ridiculous trumped-up charge of failure to identify, but the additional time I spent there was for violations that weren't even mine. I didn't even come remotely close to fitting the description of the person in the paperwork, but they wanted me there so I had to stay there regardless of what the facts were. Actually, now that I think about it, there is <u>one</u> place I don't look like I'm supposed to be… and that place is jail! That's a place that robs you of your dignity and zaps every ounce of your self-worth when you're there for doing absolutely nothing wrong.

I had gotten to know one of the other more experienced detainees while I was there and I mentioned to him that the person in my paperwork wasn't me. He was a colorful character—the kind you'd expect to see in one of those Blaxploitation movies. He seemed to know the ins and outs of the system and quickly advised me not to say anything until I was on the other side of the bars. So I took his advice and didn't say anything before my release. Looking back, I have to admit he was right. It's best to stay perfectly still when your hand is in the mouth of a sleeping lion. I had no idea what time it was when I was released. When I walked outside it was dark and at that moment it occurred to me that no one knew I'd been released. It was approximately 10:30pm and I was thinking to myself, "how am I gonna get home". I decided to take a cab back to the school and get my car. During the cab ride, my excitement to be out of jail faded fast. When we arrived on campus, all the memories of what had happened rushed back into my mind and all the anger, frustration, and feelings of uncertainty consumed me.

The day after my release, I gave the paperwork to my attorney and attempted to move on with life as best I could. It was tough! At school, I felt like a spectacle. Each day was more difficult than the one before. Everything was crashing down on me. I had academic pressure, the pressure of trying to be there for my family and look after them while struggling beneath the weight of the litigation process. Before long, it had taken a serious toll on me. I was having difficulty sleeping, I was angry all the time, it was a struggle to just function normally day to day. The stress from the lawsuit and everything surrounding it spilled over into my family and personal life and there was nothing I could do to stop it. I was powerless. I was mad all the time. The whole incident and subsequent events were wearing me down and I didn't know how to stop it and regain control of my life.

There came a point where I didn't know if I could maintain my sanity through the whole thing and my doctor put me on antidepressants, which is something I never thought I'd have to do. Then, my doctor determined that the medication wasn't achieving the desired results, so I had to make the difficult decision to start seeing a counselor to help me try and work through everything. At first, I was a little embarrassed and ashamed to admit that I needed to seek professional help to cope with the trauma of the whole ordeal. I had always considered myself a pretty strong person and the thought of any situation getting the better of me never crossed my mind. But when you face a personal attack that you don't deserve, and it's one that degrades and lowers your value as a human being, it does something to you. It has a very negative effect on many areas of your life. So I started seeing a counselor and the sessions were honest and very intimate. On several occasions, I broke down in tears because I was overwhelmed with everything—the pressure of school, the lawsuit, family, and feeling as though no one understood what I was going through. I hadn't done anything wrong and I didn't understand why I was being persecuted. What was my infraction? What was my offense? What crime had I committed to warrant such harsh treatment? The only thing I was guilty of was being born with dark skin. I'm sure most people would say, "Yeah, that's messed up, but hey that's life, sh*t happens, get over it." I suppose that could have been my attitude toward the whole situation too if it was happening to somebody else. When it's somebody else, it's very easy to say but when it's happening to you it sure isn't easy to do. No matter how strong you think you are, when you've been hurt and demeaned to that degree you can't just dust yourself off and move on as though nothing happened. Even if you put on a happy face for the outside world, deep down inside you're still struggling with the hurt.

During my sessions with the counselor I came to realize that there's no shame in knowing when you're on overload and need help coping. The sessions were very helpful. We discussed everything, my upbringing, likes and dislikes and worked our way up to the incidents. During some of the sessions I broke down in tears because I was so overwhelmed and hurt. Discussing what happened was extremely difficult because it seemed like I was reliving the encounter every time we talked about it and that was painful. These sessions helped me cope with everything that was happening to me. There's a belief among many minorities, men especially, that you're supposed to handle all your problems on your own no matter how overwhelmed or close to the edge you feel. Some believe it's a sign of weakness to seek help outside yourself. But that isn't the case at all. It takes a strong person with a keen sense of self-awareness to admit they've reached their emotional capacity. And that's where I was. Don't ever feel as though you have to be a perpetual Rock of Gibraltar; give yourself permission to be human and admit that sometimes you can't bear the weight of adversity all alone. You'll be glad you did. I'm not what you'd call an overly-emotional person; in fact, I used to wonder why people would get so emotional and all choked-up over things that happened years ago. Now I realize how tough it can be to re-live things that were painful regardless of how long ago it might have been. Wounds need time to heal and, oftentimes, even after the pain subsides there's still a scar left as a reminder. Sometimes looking at the scar takes you back to that place in time and you remember how intense the pain was when you suffered the injury. That's what happens to me whenever something reminds me of my ordeal—I re-live it all over again and it's as fresh in my mind as it was when it happened. But it's not good to focus on the pain or the scar too long because there comes a time when you need to focus on healing, and do your best to move on and not join forces with the adversary who's trying to break you and bring you down. If you let it hurt you and hold you back too long then your opponent is winning. I admit I was close to the breaking point many times while balancing my obligation to my family, school and enduring the added mental and emotional exhaustion of the litigation. But, even though my strength was failing, I had to keep going because I didn't want to strengthen my opponent by giving up the fight for justice I was seeking.

8

DEPOSITIONS, ROUND TWO

Interestingly, the judge allowed us to roll both the first and second police incidents, including my wrongful arrest, into the same case so there was no need to address each issue as a separate case. I had never met the state attorney general before but my attorney forewarned me about what to expect at the deposition. I knew it would be brutal because my attorney explained that they would try to provoke me and paint me as an aggressive, easily agitated, angry black man, so I had to be prepared. The day I went to depose, something had gone wrong there in the state's office, and my attorney and I could hear the state's attorney yelling and screaming at his colleagues. I don't know what it was all about but, ultimately, that deposition was cancelled for that day and another one was scheduled.

My attorney and I arrived for the rescheduled deposition and by that time, I had graduated. During the proceedings, my attorney requested that the state's attorney address me as Dr. Arnette but he refused, which I thought was immature, unprofessional and petty, but it let me know exactly what I was dealing with. Things started out simple enough but then they quickly took a turn toward the ridiculous. The state brought up minor stuff like me parking in the visitor's parking lot when I wasn't supposed to. The state's attorney also brought up my credit card infractions and the minor traffic ticket violations I got as a kid. Apparently, he felt that bringing those things into the proceedings would show that I was someone who frequently broke the law. The whole thing plummeted to the lowest level of absurdity. But, that was part of their strategy. Then came the really fun part where he was reading back my account of what transpired. He said, "I see here where you said the officer called you a uppity nigger." I figured after I answered the question that would be it and we would move on. Wrong! He hammered and harangued on that one topic over and over. He even took it to another level and said stuff like, "When did he call you a nigger? Did he call you a nigger when you got in the car? Are you sure he even called you a nigger? Do you use the word nigger?" I mean, he went on and on until his words were just ringing in my ears. It took every ounce of strength I could muster to keep from leaping up and doing something I'd regret later on.

Prior to the deposition, I checked in with my friend's agent—I'd been keeping him informed on what was going on in the case. His advice was simple and to the point; he said, "You need to be Billy Dee Williams cool." That was good advice because I knew I had to reach deep down and find that trademark Billy Dee Williams brand of cool and believe me... it wasn't easy. My attorney knew me but he really didn't know the depth of my resolve. I believe he was as upset and annoyed by the Attorney General as I was. I was simmering and trying my hardest not to reach the boiling point. My attorney sensed that and asked the moderator if we could take a break. During the break, my attorney said, "Don, you gotta keep it together, just stay calm." If someone had told me years earlier that I'd be in the forefront of a case like this I wouldn't have believed them. Taking a stand in the face of injustice is definitely difficult, but <u>not</u> taking a stand is even more damaging in the long run because you can lose a part of yourself and your self-respect, and it doesn't send a very good message to the younger generation.

After the break, we went back in and once the state's attorney realized he wasn't going to get the reaction from me he wanted, he backed off a bit and the process continued to move along. You see, you have to rise above what's expected of you. The state's attorney did his best to provoke me into becoming the belligerent, confrontational, angry black man they made me out to be, but I wouldn't give him the satisfaction. I refused to pour myself into the mold that he and others in society have carved out for young black men.

More than once, I teetered on the edge of my breaking point, but I kept it together. It would have been nice if the whole thing could have been done and over with quickly, but even though that particular hurdle was jumped it wasn't over yet.

9

MAKING
HEADLINES

The old adage—*'when it rains it pours'* could not have been truer at that time in my life. There were so many things happening all at once. I felt like I was in a never-ending dream that sometimes evolved into a nightmare. My head was spinning all the time. I was constantly braced for the next unexpected broadside. At the outset, I never imagined my civil rights case would be ongoing for so long—actually, I had no idea it would turn into such a momentous event. Then, on the heels of all the legal proceedings, a reporter came to campus to interview Dr. Cryer, who was in charge of minority student affairs and recruitment of minority students. The purpose of the interview, initially, was to discuss the Hopwood vs. State of Texas decision and the subsequent abolition of affirmative action in Texas universities. The reporter wanted Dr. Cryer's input as to how the outcome of that case had affected minority student enrollment. At some point during the interview, my name came up and suddenly, out of the blue, I started getting calls from a reporter. When I told my attorney about the reporter requesting an interview with me, my attorney advised me not to do the interview because he didn't want our case litigated in the media. So, over and over, I declined to talk to the reporter. Finally, the reporter told me he was doing the story either way—with or without my input. That put me in a dicey situation because he essentially said he would write the article giving the police department's account of what happened, which would not have made me look very good at all. The article would have described me as a belligerent, aggressive, angry black man—according to police, and the reporter would have ended with, 'Dr. Arnette had no comment.' I explained to my attorney that I didn't want to be shown in a bad light without giving my side of the story. So, he reluctantly agreed that I could do the interview. As interviews go, I suppose it went as well as could be expected considering the subject matter. I was, however, somewhat peeved with the fact that they couldn't just do the article about the current events, they had to throw something negative in there. The article mentioned that old credit card case from when I was a teenager, which I thought was kind of tacky but they, apparently, didn't want to shine too bright of a light on me they had to make sure I was slightly tarnished. But... what do you do? You move on.

A short time later, my son and I were in the check-out line at the grocery store, and he was doing his usual inventory-ing of the candy rack to be sure they were well-stocked. The candy happened to be right by the newspapers and magazines, and my son glanced over at them and said, "Daddy, look, that's you!" I looked over and, sure enough, I was on the front page of the Sunday paper with a head-line that read: *Medical School Accused of Racial Profiling*. I must admit they did a pretty good job of outlining and telling the story in general, even with the mention of my past infractions it was still a good article. One significant paragraph went as follows:

School leaders caution against assuming that the charges in the lawsuit are either legitimate or representative of daily life at UT Southwestern.

"It would be a leap in the reasoning process to assume that the allegations are correct, if the facts haven't been verified," said Mr. Bode, UT Southwestern's spokesman.

But after the Feb. 2 incident, at least six students - blacks and Hispanics - wrote e-mails to school officials describing experiences of possible racial profiling by police.

Steve Clark, a black fourth-year medical student, said he was frequently stopped his first two years, when medical students typically do not wear lab coats. One weekday afternoon, Mr. Clark was studying in a lab carrel, logged onto a computer, with his physiology books open. A campus officer walked by and asked if he was a student. When

Mr. Clark answered yes, the officer then asked to see his ID badge.

"Do I get the sense that he did that because I was black? Yes, I did," Mr. Clark told The News.

"I mean I'm sitting there, logged into a computer with my medical books open. What about that does not say medical student - besides the fact that I might be black?"

Dr. Cryer has talked to other minority students with similar experiences.

"They would be singled out, asked for identification, sometimes multiple forms of identification, and then have the identification scrutinized. They would be followed by police cars as they walked to or from the parking garage," he said. "Another recurring theme is for the police officer to ask for backup."

All along the opposing side was trying to imply that I was

making the whole thing up because I was just an angry black man with an axe to grind. But the article clearly stated that other minority students had experienced similar events. So it was very refreshing and uplifting to have my claims verified and validated by other students I didn't even know.

Naturally, I grabbed a few papers for posterity. Shortly after the article hit the newsstands, the university president sent out an email blast to everyone saying, in essence, that the university was not guilty of any wrongdoing regardless of what was stated in the article. That was a rather disappointing blow to me because if the university hadn't done anything wrong then the email was implying that I was overreacting or flat-out lying about the events, which I was not.

Regardless of what was going on around me, I had to keep moving forward with life, and trying my best to stay on track. As strange as it may seem, I accepted a fellowship from UT Southwestern even though my civil rights case was still open and ongoing. I'd had other offers for fellow-ships from other institutions so I had the option to go else-where, but by then it had become so personal for me that I had to show them I wasn't that easy to get rid of. I was still there pursuing my education and they hadn't chased me away, although it seemed like someone was trying to. As a fellow, I was paid once a month. Then suddenly, I didn't receive a check for two months. When I inquired I was told it was an accounting oversight, which coincidentally oc-curred just after the newspaper article hit the street. To me, the timing of the accounting glitch seemed a little too co-incidental, but they eventually straightened it out and the world kept turning. Then other things started happening. My truck was mysteriously stolen and stripped. Witnesses said they saw a tow truck near my vehicle, which was in an area that tow trucks would never have gone. Then I got a phone call from a security guard one day who claimed they had a picture of me on a dartboard down at the po-lice station. The security guard also said they were under specific orders not to engage with me under any circum-stances. Police officers and security guards for the university met in the same building and had joint meetings from time to time. I started getting tons of letters from people I didn't know, some of them were letters of support but some weren't. Civil rights cases such as mine seem to attract all kinds of people. For the most part, the majority had positive things to say, but there's always that cluster of cave-dwellers who just want to spout their negative drivel. It was a little unsettling, to say the least, but I didn't allow it to dissuade me because I knew I had to keep moving forward.

10

MEDIATION
– THE LAST LAP

My attorney and I went to Austin for mediation. He told me not to expect much because the mediation process was basically just each side giving a summary of their case. There wasn't necessarily any new information to provide, we were just recapping and presenting our case before the mediator. It ended up being an all-day affair. We arrived about 7:30 a.m. and were there until about 6:30 p.m.

Much to my chagrin, the same representative for the state who reveled in his N-word dissertation, was among those in attendance at mediation. He had no qualms about describing me as a criminal trying to take advantage of the system just to make a buck, which was beyond ridiculous and insulting because nothing could have been farther from the truth. As a matter of fact, my attorney later said that he didn't take my case because of any monetary gain, he took it because it was the right thing to do. Doing the right thing had been my guiding force all along, I wasn't interested in monetary gain either. I was interested in fairness, equality, justice and basic human consideration and mutual respect. I don't think that's an unreasonable expectation. If I were only after money, I wouldn't have suffered all the anxiety and emotional trauma caused by the police incidents, the filing of the lawsuit and all the proceedings that followed. The fact that the whole thing affected me so deeply and personally is an indication that it wasn't about money. But of course, the state's attorney's job is to strengthen their case by trying to weaken ours.

After a long tiring day, an offer to settle was put on the table, and my attorney advised that we accept the offer or be prepared to spend another three to four years tied up in litigation. He warned me about how these cases could drag on and on, especially when you factor in all the appeals. Even if I won the case outright, the state could 'and would' appeal that decision, which would just keep prolonging the case indefinitely. It had already been a long, emotionally draining process and it just seemed like it was time to put the whole thing to rest. So, we accepted the offer, although I had mixed emotions about it. I felt a modicum of relief that it was over, but at the same time I also felt like I was letting a lot of people down. I had become the voice for many other minorities who had gone through similar situations and were rooting for me to stay the course and keep going. By accepting a settlement, I couldn't help but feel as though I betrayed those people. By the time we reached the mediation process, the case had adversely affected every area of my life; my family, my enthusiasm and zeal for my education, relationships on and off campus—it took an enormous toll on me and it was time to move on.

After everything was over, I still had lingering doubts as to whether I had really accomplished anything; whether I'd made a difference significant enough to have a positive impact on the lives of others. Then one day, I was at a shopping mall and a gentleman came up to me and said, "You're Dr. Arnette, aren't you?" I said, 'Yes.' He told me he was a police officer at UT Southwestern, and then he said something that genuinely humbled me. He said, "I want to thank you because it wasn't until you did what you did that things started to change." It was heartwarming to hear. He went on to say, "The old police chief was fired and African Americans are being put in more positions of authority." Among other things, he said much of the harassing of minority students has stopped. We spoke for a good while and after we each went on with our day, I said to myself, '*Wow, I did make a difference.*' Then I knew it was all worth it.

By no means am I trying to paint a negative picture of UT Southwestern; it's one of the finest universities in the world and I owe much of my success to that institution. I had a good rapport with all the faculty and administration. But there were disparities that were completely unrelated and exclusive of academia that needed to be brought to the forefront and addressed, so that the field could be leveled for all students regardless of the color of their skin.

It's worth mentioning that according to the Journal of Blacks in Higher Education, black enrollment increased from twenty-one students in 1999 to fifty-five students in 2004, which they state was the fastest rate of increase among the top twenty-five medical schools in the country. So, even as the lawsuit was going on we were making strides, and changes in the status quo were taking place. One person can be the catalyst to groundbreaking progress.

So I say to young people who don't know how to handle disrespect, this is how you fight. You don't fight injustice by reacting violently or behaving the way society expects you to behave. You fight by pushing through all the obstacles and blockades placed in your way. You fight by becoming a success in spite of the odds being against you. You fight by saying, 'hey, the majority of the masses thought I couldn't make it but I did.' You fight by holding people accountable the right way, and by doing so, no matter the outcome you still win.

During the litigation process, I did a lot of soul-searching and reflecting on many different things. I thought about where I was in life and where I was going. I thought about defining moments and people who had significantly changed the trajectory of my life.

It was during this journey of self-discovery that I wrote the following poem:

Sometimes I wonder where I'd be

If it wasn't for the kindness of Melanie

She gave me a once in a lifetime chance

Which I took advantage of now I'm a successful man

Without Melanie's guidance to direct me

I think I would have fallen short of my possibilities

I would have never reached my full potential

But thanks to her I now have credentials

I've gone on to be the first ever on different occasions

One first was a wonderful achievement

While the other first brought me much grief

With the good times also come the bad times

Which is okay because sometimes that's the cost to be the

first of your kind

No matter what people say or do

I will continue to be honest and true

At times it's very difficult to turn the other cheek

But in the end the taste of victory will be oh so sweet

Melanie Cobb has done so much for me

Without her, I would not have my doctorate degree

11

MOVING ON

It was 2006, and with the lawsuit behind me it was time to press on. I had successfully completed my education, graduated and did my post-doctorate fellowship at UT Southwestern. I was officially the first African American man to graduate in my discipline from the medical school, and it was quite an honor. No, there was no parade, no special accolades or tributes given to me for that historic accomplishment, but that was okay because I knew I had accomplished what I set out to do and that was enough. I do, however, find it troubling that it was 2005 before an African American male graduated from that institution in my discipline. That's a sad commentary on so many different levels. Are we allowing others to hold us back? Are we holding ourselves back to some degree? There could be multiple answers to those questions, so each individual has to do their own soul-searching and realize what's true in their case.

At any rate, I knew I had to keep moving forward so I endeavored to claim or 'reclaim' the areas of my life that had been virtually consumed by the conflicts and legal proceedings of the previous years. After completing my fellowship at UT Southwestern, I journeyed on to Yale, which just happened to be Dr. Ben Carson's Alma Mater. I had been greatly inspired by reading his books when I was in ninth grade, and years later, there I was walking the same campus. While I was there, the pharmaceutical companies began to entice me away from the traditional hospital setting. They were convinced, and subsequently convinced me, that my talents could be better utilized on a more global scale rather than limited to a local area. That concept definitely piqued my interest because it was an opportunity for me to make a difference in a broader sense by affecting the quality of life for people worldwide, which is exactly what I wanted to do. So I accepted a position with

Bristol-Myers Squibb in the medical affairs department. I was the go-to guy in the southeast region of the country and I loved it. For the most part, my role was working on clinical trials and drug development as well as consulting and giving data about the various new drugs to physicians. I was what you would call a medical liaison. I acted as a conduit between the pharmaceutical company and the physician. We're all well aware of the fact that doctors play a major role in the health and wellbeing of their patients, and sometimes the results of various clinical drug trials aren't always readily available to physicians. So they rely heavily on information provided by pharmaceutical companies to assess the benefit of a particular drug for their patient based upon data that resulted from the clinical trial. That's when the role of *medical liaison* becomes vital. It was a key part of my job in the medical affairs department. A doctor's decision as to whether they should prescribe or not prescribe a certain drug often hinged on the information they'd get from me. Obviously, the final decision rests with the physician, but the pharmaceutical company plays a critical role in providing the doctor with pertinent data that will aid him or her in making the right decision for their patient.

It's safe to say that the population at large gives very little thought to things that have been around for ages, such as prescription medication. You go to the doctor for whatever ails you; you get a prescription, you take your medication and as long as you get the desired results, you move on with life without giving any more thought to how much time and energy went into the development of that drug. The average person has no inkling of how multidimensional and complex the field of Pharmacology really is. It is a significant, ever-changing and evolving branch of medicine that focuses not only on the development of drugs but on their action in the human body and interaction with other pharmaceuticals. We're developing new drugs all the time, especially in the field of oncology.

My hope is that more minorities (and even those who are not minorities but are considered unlikely candidates for whatever reason) will start to branch out into careers and professions that have historically not been held by that particular demographic. There's a tremendous need to diversify medicine and give more attention to specific health issues that plague certain groups of the population — African Americans in particular, which I'll talk more about later.

When I was hired as a medical liaison with Bristol-Myers Squibb, I was one of only forty-eight people nationwide who held that particular job. Once again, I found myself in a minority of one because I was the only African American in my particular division. By that time, I was used to standing out like the proverbial sore thumb so it was nothing new and really didn't bother me. I acclimated relatively quickly to the professional climate and had a number of memorable and meaningful experiences while I was there — some were even kind of comical. Case in point: As a general rule, I'm a rather meticulous person when it comes to how I dress for work. One time my director and I were talking and she said, "Don, you have to stop telling people how much you pay for your clothes." My response was, "I don't know what you mean by that, what are you talking about?" She proceeded to reiterate that I shouldn't tell people how much my clothes cost. I was puzzled for a minute then I realized what was going on. There were several occasions when people would compliment me on what I was wearing—saying things like, "That's a really nice shirt you're wearing, how much does a shirt like that cost?" I'd usually say something like, "Oh, it's not too bad." And as the conversation would progress the person might say something like, "I know those shirts aren't cheap" or something to that effect. It was astounding how a simple statement could get twisted and converted into something it wasn't. There's a saying that if you line five people up and tell the first person something is blue, by the time they pass it down to the fifth person it's red.

We'd have these national meetings that were four or five days long and I'd be the only one who wore a different suit every day. It's not often someone comes under fire for being too stylish. Of all things to be reprimanded for, being a snazzy dresser would be the last thing you'd expect. Sometimes even when you do all the right things, say all the right things, and wear all the right things you can still be met with opposition. But that doesn't matter; you have to continue to do all the right things. Make absolutely sure that whatever adversity you encounter was not caused by anything you did wrong. I'm not criticizing any of my colleagues who chose to dress as they dressed; whatever works for them works for them, but it doesn't work for me. Every individual is different and we each have to decide what image we want to project.

I worked for Bristol-Myers Squibb for five years and I was very grateful for that opportunity. Then I journeyed on to a smaller company before ultimately landing at Onyx Pharmaceuticals, which is a company dedicated to the development of medicine to aid in the treatment of cancer. When I started, Dr. Tony Coles was CEO. He's an African American man with a bigger eye for fashion than mine. This company was a Godsend because I was in my element. Dr. Coles was an eloquent, charismatic, articulate, equally snazzy dresser whose personal persona exemplified class and intellect. It felt great to be in the company of someone who thought like me and best of all, looked like me. Dr. Coles was a true role model for me. He was a trailblazer in many respects. We seldom find men of his caliber. I don't mean just in minority circles but multi-cultural circles. However, that doesn't mean they're not out there, they're definitely out there and we need to emulate them so the generation after us will have strong examples and role models to follow. Dr. Coles eventually moved on to his next venture but his reputation and the footprints he left linger on. To follow in the footsteps of men like that is a distinct privilege because if that becomes the model and the norm, it'll soon be commonplace to see minorities in esteemed positions of authority.

My clinical and research work is something I'm very passionate about because of the necessity to address unmet medical needs—especially those affecting minority communities. For example, diabetes impacts the African American community at a much higher rate than other communities. I spoke at length about the incidence of diabetes and its indicators in my 2005 dissertation. In addition to that, one of the main reasons I chose to do my fellowship at UT Southwestern was because of an in-depth heart study they were doing to assess the risk factors for heart disease, and I wanted to help push along the research in that area. Most studies about heart disease and risk factors are based upon the Framingham Heart Study, which spanned over decades and provided invaluable data. However, every participant in that particular study was Caucasian, therefore it didn't specifically address those risks that are only applicable to African Americans and other minorities. Biologically speaking, African Americans have more intervening genetic issues that can affect their heart health. So I was very excited when we started a Dallas heart study because it was an opportunity to do our own risk assessment that could prove to be more applicable to minorities.

Given the fact that genetic profiles vary greatly in the various ethnic groups, there's a need for a tightly focused approach to specific health situations that are more prevalent in certain cultures than others. This is an issue that's near and dear to my heart because good health and good healthcare should be available for everyone, and the more we know about what affects a particular ethnic group, the better care we can provide them. Healthcare statistics suggest that the lack of minorities in medicine will prove to be problematic over time for a number of reasons. One of the main concerns is that it could limit access to medical care in low-income, inner-city communities, which is a troubling yet very real possibility. However, we shouldn't focus solely on one community because you can make a universal difference if you put your mind to it. It shouldn't only be about helping your particular ethnic group; it should be about making a difference in communities at large, and improving the lives of people simply because there's a need.

I don't want it to appear that I'm pushing for young minorities to go to medical school and/or graduate school and not consider other career paths because that's not what I'm doing. I'm not solely promoting the medical field as a means for success. I'm pushing for young people from all walks of life to go beyond the corridors of limitations and aim higher than they thought they could. Sure, I'd love to see more minority medical students because it's an area in need of diversity. But the message I'm trying to send is that there's more than one road to success, and if you want to be a doctor don't allow anyone to tell you that you can't because you don't fit the mold or the acceptable profile of what a doctor (or any other professional) should look like.

12

IMPRESSIONS

Even to this day I'm still placed in a stereotypical container by those who don't know me. When people see me out and about, it's apparent to them that I'm successful based upon the vehicle I drive, the clothes I wear, my persona, etc., they just don't know what I'm successful at, but more often than not they assume I'm an athlete. The first thing they say to me is, "Hey man, you play ball?" Or "Who do you play for?" For a split second, I find it amusing and think, *'wow, so this is what it would have felt like to be a professional athlete.'* And just for a moment I'm filled with wonder as to what my life would have been like had I followed that path. But then I snap out of it and come back to reality and respond with, "Nah, man, I'm a clinical researcher" or I'll say, "I'm a doctor" or "I'm a scientist."

Their response is always the same. First there's a pause and then astonishment on their part. Most of the time they'll say, "For real?" And I'll say, 'Yep, stay in school, it pays."

Don't get me wrong, it's often flattering to be mistaken for a professional athlete. But by the same token, it's still disheartening when people are amazed that I have a different profession. The fact that I'm capable of being successful in other careers shouldn't shock people. We need to shake that mindset we've had far too long, and realize that success can come in all colors, shapes, sizes, ages, backgrounds, socioeconomic status, etc. That's the message I'm determined to convey. I'm trying not to keep harping on this subject but I'm sure by now it's become abundantly clear that I'm very passionate about this issue. Yes, it's definitely flattering that African Americans are touted as some of the best athletes. However, my point is that a tall well-groomed black man should not automatically garner the title of professional athlete because he could also be a world-class neurosurgeon or a politician or an attorney or a real estate developer or hold any number of other prestigious positions.

While I'm on the subject of appearance, I'd like to segue a bit to something I frequently caution kids about. I tell them to be mindful of how they present themselves in public, because perception is reality to those who don't know you personally. Just as I get mistaken for a professional basketball player because of my appearance, I tell kids that they, too, can be mistaken for things they're not. I tell them if you walk outside with your pants sagging, slouching around looking like a thug, you could be the smartest kid in the world but how would anyone know that? Society's first inclination will be to associate you with kids of a certain type of behavior. They'll look at you and instantly assume you're into drugs and possibly gang-affiliated. Most will be hesitant to pass you on the street and when they do, males will keep a close eye on you and females will clutch their purses tighter because you look the part. I've had many kids tell me that they don't think people should judge them by what they wear, and while that's true, I always respond to that statement by telling them they have to realize that all people have to go on is how you initially appear to be until they get to know you. The problem is will they take the time to get to know the real you? When people perceive you to be a certain type of person based upon how you presented yourself the first time they saw you, chances are they won't go out of their way to change their opinion of you. It's going to take some work on your part. There's a slogan a commercial used back in the day that says: *You never get a second chance to make a first impression.* That still rings true to this day.

I often like to use this analogy when I talk to kids: Okay, let's say you're outside and you've just been the victim of a crime, let's say you've just been robbed. You look over and there's a man in a police uniform standing not too far away. You run up to him and tell him you've just been robbed and ask for his help. He says, "Why are you telling me?" And you say, "Because you're a police officer." And he says, "I'm not a police officer." You say, "Look how you're dressed, you're dressed like a cop." And he says, "Just because I'm dressed like this doesn't mean I'm a cop." Obviously, that's an extreme scenario, but the point is kids need to be careful what uniform they wear. Is it right? Should things be that way? Probably not, but we live in a world where <u>perception</u> is <u>reality</u>. What uniform are you wearing? You don't find out the reality of who a person is until later, but perception is immediate—at first glance, and that's how you'll be judged. So I caution kids to be mindful of what image they project. It can be a constant daily struggle to rise above the labeling that young people are subjected to. Sadly, African American males face challenges that are uniquely different from those of females and males of other ethnic groups. In addition to the prevailing public perception, young black males also struggle with self-perception, which often mirrors society's views and is therefore counterproductive.

In an earlier chapter, I talked about how young black males often think they can only be successful if they pursue sports or music, but I tend to campaign hard against that belief. Once again, I'm not taking anything away from the amazing minority athletes out there. What I'm saying is we need to stop putting African Americans in a success box labeled 'athletes and musicians', because that's not the only avenue you can take to succeed. There's also a widespread assumption that when young black athletes go to college, they get in based solely upon their athletic ability and not their academic aptitude.

Generally speaking, society has ingrained stereotypical thinking so deep into the minds of young minorities that many won't even strive for greater accomplishments; they have tunnel vision and at the end of the tunnel all they see is sports or music. I remember once when I was speaking to a group of kids, a little girl about nine or ten years old said to me, "You can't be a doctor because you have tattoos." That child's statement is proof-positive that we have set mental boundaries as to what a certain group of people can or cannot be based upon who they are and how they look. I always try my best to dispel that notion to everyone who crosses my path. There's much to be done in our communities and so much potential locked away in young minds, if only they'd recognize it and stop putting limitations on themselves they could accomplish more than they ever imagined was possible.

13

DEFYING
THE ODDS

I'd like to talk a little bit about the inspiration for the title of this book; _I AM supposed to be here_. Having read through the earlier chapters you may have already surmised that the title was born out of the statement the officer made to me on UT Southwestern's campus. It resonated with me then, and to this day it still gives me pause when I think about being told that I didn't look like I was supposed to be there. Down through history people have defied the odds and dared to go beyond the limitations put on them by society. So, with that in mind, let's look at several people who didn't look like they were supposed to be where they ended up. Let's start with our current president. As a child, a teenager, a young adult, President Obama most definitely didn't look like he'd ever hold the office of president of the United States, and yet not only was he elected in 2008, he was re-elected and won a second term in 2012. President Obama is from humble beginnings. His mother grew up in Wichita, KS, where her father worked on oil rigs and her mother worked on an assembly line during the great depression. The president's father was born in Kenya and grew up herding goats. President Obama was quoted as saying he never knew or had a relationship with his father, and life circumstances made it necessary for him to live with his grandparents. His start in life was less-than-ideal but he had dreams, ambition and goals that drove him to educate himself and not give up. His drive and determination landed him the best seat in the White House. When he was just another young black man walking down the street, he didn't look like he'd end up being the 44th president of the United States.

And then there's Carol Bartz, former CEO of Yahoo. Her mother died when Carol was only eight years old. She and her younger brother were sent to live with her grandmother on a dairy farm in Wisconsin. Her life is a perfect example of a less-than-ideal start, and yet she educated herself and went on to become a top-level executive at numerous technological conglomerates, ultimately being named CEO of Yahoo. Many would have said because of her start in life, maybe even because of her gender, she didn't look like she belonged in such a high-ranking position.

Being a black female born in rural Mississippi, I'm sure Oprah Winfrey didn't look like she would become a media giant but she did. Not only that, according to Forbes magazine, Oprah was the richest African American of the 20th century and the world's only black billionaire. She's been named the most influential woman of her generation. Before she achieved her level of success, I'd venture to say no one thought she'd accomplish as much as she has.

Oscar Pistorius was born with a congenital defect in both his legs, which ultimately caused his legs to be amputated below his knees. With his physical challenges early in life, who would ever have imagined that he would become an award-winning Olympic Sprinter? He was once asked what his motto was and he said: "You're not disabled by the disabilities you have, you're able by the abilities you have."

There's a teacher named Brad Cohen who was born in St. Louis, MO, and diagnosed with Tourette Syndrome at the age of twelve. Mayo Clinic describes Tourette Syndrome as a nervous system (neurological) disorder that starts in childhood. It involves unusual repetitive movements or unwanted sounds that can't be controlled (tics). For instance, you may repeatedly blink your eyes, shrug your shoulders or jerk your head. In some cases, you might unintentionally blurt out offensive words. Brad Cohen used to bark and twitch uncontrollably and you can imagine the ridicule and humiliation he endured at school. Most kids with his condition would have withdrawn and settled into a life of defeat, but not Brad, he triumphed over his disorder and went on to graduate cum laude from Bradley University where he majored in elementary education. He earned many academic honors, and after being turned down twenty-four times for teaching positions, he finally landed a job teaching third and fourth grade. As of 2013, he was assistant vice principal of an elementary school in Georgia. You wouldn't expect someone with his challenges to accomplish so much. He's a motivational speaker, teacher, school administrator, and author. He most definitely did not look like he was supposed to be there.

Liz Murray is another example of someone who didn't look like she was supposed to be where she was [and is]. Her life story was the inspiration behind the TV movie, *"Homeless to Harvard."* Her parents were both drug addicts and she and her sister often went days without food. After years of neglect and hopelessness, she left home at age fifteen. Her mother died of AIDS, and her father also succumbed to the same deadly disease years later. She spent much of her adolescence couch-hopping at different friends' homes. She slept in stairwells, on subway trains and even on the street. Liz Murray's story could have had a very different ending. She could have become another tragic statistic, another victim of street life. But she wanted something more. She defied the odds and instead of becoming a victim of her circumstances, she won a scholarship to Harvard University and graduated in 2009.

Defying the odds and daring to succeed in the face of adversity is not a new concept; it transcends all cultures and has always existed in the human spirit, but it's often suppressed or buried beneath fear of failure. Over a hundred years ago Helen Keller, who was deaf and blind earned a college degree. She went on to write twelve books and was also a social activist campaigning for women's rights. Look at all the strikes she had against her. She was a female during a time when women had very few rights; she was deaf and she was blind, yet she accomplished great things and her legacy and memory live on today.

Ordinary people can do extraordinary things. The first thing you need is the desire to succeed. You may be a clerk or an administrative assistant with aspirations to be among the top-level executives. You may think you'd look out-of-place seated at the head of the conference table, or in board meetings making major company decisions. You may think someone who looks like you couldn't possibly belong in a position like that, and maybe a few people have made you feel you don't belong. But, just because you don't look like you're supposed to be somewhere doesn't mean you're not supposed to be there! If you have a desire to succeed, success can be yours.

It doesn't matter what walk of life or life circumstance you happen to be in, you still have the right to dream. You have the right to be ambitious and get to where you want to be in life. It's unfortunate, but mainstream society has a way of making you feel you don't belong in a certain place or in a certain classification because it isn't the norm to see people like you holding traditional upper-level positions. The muddy waters of discrimination run deep and cover a broad gamut of life situations. Sometimes you're ostracized based on race; sometimes it's class; sometimes it's gender; it could be age in other cases; it could even be because of a physical or mental challenge that causes you to buy into the predominant opinion that you don't belong. When it rears its ugly head, it isn't always blatant in-your-face bigotry. More often than not, it's covertly concealed and cleverly hidden under the guise of something else. For example, in my case, I was told that I didn't look like I was supposed to be there because apparently I didn't look like a student. Why not? Why didn't I fit the profile of a student? I was neatly dressed, walking toward one of the buildings on campus, and minding my own business just like the other students. The only difference was I wasn't the same color as the other students. In other cases, people have been told in a "politically correct" manner that they're not right for a certain job or other opportunity. The powers-that-be have a multitude of bogus reasons they'll give you when in reality they just don't think you look the part. If they were to tell you the truth, they'd say you're too old or too young or the wrong gender or the wrong color or you're too thin or too thick. That's not likely to happen these days because of the threat of a lawsuit being filed against them. But the fact that it's unspoken doesn't mean it doesn't exist. If you've ever been pushed aside and counted out for the reasons I've mentioned or for any other reason, don't give up. Never give up! Do not succumb to someone else's belief that you don't belong. It's not okay and it's not acceptable to be denigrated and dismissed simply because of how you look or because of your place and circumstance in life. You don't have to just roll over and accept it as your lot in life. Another thing, don't confuse feelings with facts. If someone's made you feel like a failure or like you'll never reach a certain point, that doesn't make it a fact. It's not true unless you allow it to be true by yielding and surrendering to how they've made you think and feel about yourself. Don't do it. Don't pour yourself into the mold mainstream society has designed for you.

Stereotyping in its purest form, I believe, is mainstream society's reluctance to deal with each person on an individual basis. It amounts to social laziness. It's so much easier to just bundle people into a group and not address them as one separate human being because that takes the pressure off the one with the negative stereotypical viewpoint. They don't have to make a concerted effort to assess you as a person, they can just lump you into a herd of people they already have a label for. I don't think anyone's hands are sparkling clean in this regard, to some degree, we've all been guilty of social lethargy and apathy.

Sometimes it takes confidence and a belief in yourself first, and then others will believe in you. That was the case for me. Dr. Cobb believed in me because she saw potential in me that I might not have even realized I had at that time. I entered that program with quite a bit of trepidation, and I didn't have a very strong belief in my ability to succeed. But she did, and that motivated me and helped boost my confidence in myself. As I said in an earlier chapter, I persevered also because I didn't want to let Dr. Cobb down since she was rooting for me. Our young people need strong role models and examples to follow. We've heard people jokingly say, *there's no I in team but there's a me*. Well, I have another one, *there's no I in success but there's an us*. Keep in mind that your success is like a stream, it flows through many different areas of your life. It impacts everyone in your circle and beyond. It obviously has a positive effect on your family but it can also have a positive effect on your community. You could be the role model and example others in your community want to emulate. So never give up and settle for less than you're capable of just because you've been made to think you're wrapped in the wrong kind of skin.

14

LEARNING FROM TRAGEDY

As of the writing of this book another senseless tragedy oc-
curred, this time in Ferguson, MO. A young African American man was shot and killed by a police officer. Anytime
a life is lost, no matter what the mitigating circumstances
were surrounding the incident, it's always a tragedy. But
when a <u>young</u> life is lost it's even more devastating and
difficult to accept because everything that young person
could have been died with them and is forever lost. All
the things they could have accomplished for themselves
and for mankind are forever lost. We'll never know where
life would have taken them had they lived. When trage-
dies like these happen we're bombarded with a barrage

of emotions. People are angry, as evidenced by the rioting and looting that resulted from the protests. People want to know why this tragedy happened. They want justice and they want the guilty party to pay because guilt demands some kind of retribution. It's a natural human emotion to want some kind of revenge when we've been hurt. But violence is never the answer. It only makes a bad situation worse. As I mentioned earlier, certain actions can have severe consequences, and loss of life is as severe as it gets. That's why as a people we need to take a serious look at ourselves, both individually and as a community or ethnic group. We need to do some serious soul-searching to see if we may be contributing to the deterioration of our communities, and if we can be more instrumental in turning things around. It's true that sometimes no matter what you do you're still singled out because you look a certain way or live in a certain neighborhood but that doesn't mean you have to take on the image and fall into a pattern of the way society thinks you're supposed to behave.

During that first incident with the campus police I knew

I had to be calm and cool so as not to give them a reason to harm me. Granted, some don't need a reason but as minorities we need an extra dose of composure because the odds are seriously against us. When I refused to get into the elevator alone with that police officer, it was because I was keenly aware of how things are for minorities, especially males. I was thinking survival... plain and simple. Is it right that we, as minority males, have to be on our guard all the time and make sure we walk lightly in certain situations? No, it isn't right and it isn't fair... but it's life in the real world. It's a fact. It's about survival. Simply put, you want to walk away from the encounter with your life. If at some point you want to seek justice because you feel profiled or disrespected, do it through the proper channels — utilize the justice system, that's why it's there. No, the system isn't perfect and there's no guarantee you'll prevail, but that's the proper way to fight. Each time you fight the proper way, you send a very clear message to society and a positive one to your community. When you take a non-violent stand it lets people know that you're a wise and credible person, and no matter the outcome you feel a little more empowered as a human being because you took the high road and didn't succumb to the tendency to respond negatively. It doesn't matter what other people are doing around you, when you do the right thing you're always the better person.

Our hearts ache for the parents and family of every young person who has lost their life tragically, whether it's as a result of senseless violence or as in the Ferguson, MO case. Either way, we mourn for them. But reacting violently never solved anything it only brings more heartache and pain. Violence begets violence and it trickles into every crevice of the community. All it does is further perpetuate the stereotype that African Americans are angry, violent gangsters and thugs that no one should care about anyway. As long as we fulfill that mindset we're doing a tremendous disservice to our children and young people in general, not to mention the terrible disservice we're doing to the memory of those who have gone before us. Think of all the civil rights activists who lost their lives fighting to pave the way for a better life for their children and for their people. Without question there have been many great leaders of all creeds and colors down through history, but at the moment I'm speaking specifically about African American frontrunners who paid the ultimate price in an effort to smooth out the rough road and secure some kind of equality for blacks in the U.S.

We owe it to ourselves and to our children to be the best we can be. But in addition to that, we owe it to the memory of those men and women who lost their lives fighting for our civil rights. We should honor their memories and their sacrifices.

Our response to adversity is extremely important. Not only does it play a big part in determining if you'll get the results or outcome you seek but it can also impact the likelihood of a particular incident happening again. We should always try to look at the big picture and think long and hard before we respond. I know that may be easier said than done but decisions made while we are emotional can have very negative results. In my situation, I decided to file a lawsuit, I thought that course of action would give me the best opportunity to shine a light on issues that were occurring and try to reduce the possibility that the same thing would happen to others.

We don't have all the facts that contributed to the tragedy in Ferguson but we all know the subsequent outcome. I've seen the community ban together in numerous protests to show their anger and frustration. Let me ask this question, is a protest enough? I would say, no. We need to look at problems on a more global level. If the people in Ferguson don't like the police officers then that means they don't like the police department. How do you address that? You start by voting new local political leaders into office—from the mayor to city council members. I think the protests could have also been an opportunity to increase voter registration and begin to repair the damage at a civil level. The officer in question will get his day in court but the community should be focusing more on how we can show our local officials that this type of tragedy should never happen again. In this instance, it's better to fight with your vote!

When faced with any type of conflict, you should first assess the incident as a whole. Ask yourself if there's anything you can do differently to avoid a consequential negative outcome. Then determine what result will be in your best interest, and the best interest of all parties involved. And most importantly, how are you going to achieve your result. You always have to make sure you 'fight' the right way. There are multiple methods of fighting the right way: Courtrooms, boycotts, protests, the voting booth, just to name a few. You have to take a non-violent approach to combating injustice, otherwise you lose credibility and you defeat your own purposes. Remember, emotions are a natural response to both good things and bad things. BUT, decisions based on emotions typically don't have the best outcomes.

15

OWNERSHIP OF OUR ACTIONS

What do I mean by ownership of our actions? I mean every individual has to take ownership of their actions and their re-actions and never seek to shift the blame onto the shoulders of someone else. Always think about the consequences of every action you take, and realize that some actions can have pretty severe consequences—even if you felt justified in taking them. Even when the other person is just as culpable as you in the situation, you still have to choose to take the high road no matter what. Is it easy? Not always. But doing the right thing is always the right thing to do. We've become such a wrong-doing society that when someone does something right, we're so amazed it often makes the news. What has happened to a society when doing right becomes something rare and uncommon? It floors me whenever I read about some Good Samaritan who helped someone out; or about someone finding a wallet and returning it with the money still in there; or about someone buying a meal for a homeless person or some other random act of kindness. Isn't that what we're supposed to do? Shouldn't that be the norm? Why have those things become the exception instead of the rule? It's easy to go the way of the wrong-doers but it takes a strong person with character and integrity to take the high road and do the right thing. You won't always be widely-accepted when you do what's right. Sometimes you'll be ostracized as I was during the litigation. It's definitely no picnic, but you have to be unwavering because in the long run you'll be a better person and feel better about yourself.

A while back, Oprah Winfrey interviewed Al Sharpton, and during the interview he remarked about how his daughters are often ridiculed by their peers for being too intelligent. He said they're often told they're acting white because they're educated and articulate in their communication. I see that as a serious problem. Then he said, "Well, if they're acting white by exhibiting class and eloquence, what is acting black?" I'm paraphrasing slightly but that's the gist of what he said. To me, that's a disturbing commentary for a number of reasons, not the least of which is the fact that our young people are being jeered by members of their own ethnic group for wanting to rise above the mainstream stereotype. It's just as incumbent upon black people to be well-educated and intelligent as it is any other race.

The Daily Caller in South Carolina just recently ran a story with a headline that reads as follows: *High School Girl Taunted, Beaten at Bus Stop for Acting 'Too Much Like a White Person.'*

The first few lines of the article state: *A 16-year-old high school girl in Rock Hill, S.C. told police that another high school girl taunted her on a school bus and then beat her up after she got off the bus. The assailant allegedly was angry at the victim because she was behaving "too much like a white person." Both the alleged attacker and the victim are black, reports The State, a Columbia, S.C. newspaper.*

When stories like that surface, it should prompt us to take a step back and look at what's going on in our own backyard. It has to start with us. Perhaps some of the things that currently ail the black community could be alleviated with a better self-image, sense of worth and a determination to own your actions. In retrospect, maybe I could have contributed to defusing the first incident on campus if I had simply given the officer my identification when he asked for it rather than asking him why he wanted it. My "reaction" probably helped fuel his "actions". In all honesty, I could have taken steps to possibly alleviate the situation instead of challenging him. For instance, when he told me I didn't look like I was supposed to be there, I could have been astute enough to know that because of his negative perception of me I needed to do a complete 180 and respond in a totally different manner than what he expected. Even though I had a right to be insulted and upset I still could have responded in contrast to the way I did. This in no way implies that the officer was right or justified in acting the way he did, I'm simply stating that I personally could have responded a different way and possibly neutralize the whole situation. There could have been a completely different outcome had I done that. The same holds true in other life situations, such as relationships, whether business or personal. Oftentimes, husbands and wives will say hurtful things to each other in a heat of the moment impulse. Then once the volatility of the situation subsides, they feel awful about the things they said to their spouse. It also happens in business relationships and friendships. We have these knee-jerk reactions and responses, and we don't take the time to give thought to what the outcome or consequence of our actions could be. If your boss expresses some displeasure with your performance on the job, don't just storm out and say you quit, or go on Facebook and start badmouthing the company and your boss because something like that will come back to haunt you. Social media is colossal and word will get around about you faster than wildfire. Tarnishing the reputation of a current or former employer could potentially make it hard for you to find other jobs. Checking people out on social media has become so commonplace that even attorneys use it on occasions to support their cases; employers routinely use it to find out about the character of potential candidates; the government even uses it in some instances. So be very careful. A better way to respond to a job situation like that is to put a little extra effort into doing your job. Maybe come in ten or fifteen minutes earlier and show that you have the initiative to be an exemplary worker. Take constructive criticism and don't return fire. Don't fuel the flames. Don't respond by doing exactly what society expects you to do. Predictability is what spawns most stereotypes. When a certain type of behavior has been consistently associated with a particular group of people it becomes conceivably predictable and, subsequently, expected. Unfortunately, it doesn't even matter what percentage of people in that race or class exhibits unfavorable behavior—there might only be a few bad apples but society still has a tendency to blanket the entire race or culture. When it comes to categorizing people who are classified as minorities, one bad apple does indeed spoil the whole bunch. That's why it's so important to take a few minutes and think about the long-term effect of your actions. Take a step back and seriously consider what might happen if you say what you want to say, or if you do what you what to do. We have to take advantage of every opportunity to avoid conflict as much as we can, and by doing so we can dispel a significant amount of the negative perception our antagonist might have. This mindset needs to take hold and become a way of life. By the same token, don't allow the negative perception to BE your reality. We owe it to ourselves, to our children and to our communities at large.

Getting back to what I said earlier about how I could have responded differently to the officer, in both encounters, and possibly avoided the resultant conflict. In the first incident, I could have simply sucked it up and complied with his request. Even though his request was completely unreasonable I should have evaluated the situation and known that his negative perception of me was already settled and decided in his mind. Once again, as I said earlier, I should have done the exact opposite of what he expected and complied without objection. Likewise, in the second incident with the police, it probably wasn't the best idea for me to ask the officer if there was a problem. I shouldn't have said anything at all. I allowed my frustration with being profiled (when I wasn't doing anything wrong) to get the best of me. If I had taken a few minutes to think about the consequences of my actions, I would have just kept walking and he might have gone on about his business too. While there's no guarantee that it would have happened that way, I still regret not taking advantage of the opportunity to be the bigger person in that situation. Some might say (especially from a minority perspective), that they're afraid they'll appear weak if they remain passive during conflict. But in certain volatile situations choosing to be non-aggressive doesn't mean you're weak it means you're smart. Does racial profiling happen? Yes it does. Are innocent minorities stopped and detained by the police for no reason? Yes they are. It's just a fact of life and it's not within our power to change it at the moment. But what we can do is change our responses and reactions, and focus on neutralizing and not volatilizing the situation.

On a lateral note, sometimes the reason we negatively react in certain situations is because people nowadays are so easily offended. And that's not exclusive to one particular ethnic group, it applies to everyone. When someone offends us we feel disrespected, and when we feel disrespected it's like a personal attack upon our worth and value as a human being. And yes, it's upsetting and it hurts. When someone is in pain or feels offended, they have no qualms about hurting other people. Have you ever noticed how a person with a headache or toothache or some other nagging pain will lash out and almost take your head off for the smallest things? They're not thinking in terms of the other person's feelings or the fact that the other person is completely innocent, they're just in pain and don't care who else's feelings they hurt.

When someone is wounded they want to retaliate and strike back. When you feel attacked you want to attack back, it's a natural human response. But it also raises the issue about perception again. How you perceive a situation isn't necessarily what's going on. The fact that you feel disrespected or attacked doesn't mean you have to take matters into your own hands and challenge the other person, because sometimes that's just not a good idea. You need to take a deep breath; take a step back and think about possible outcomes.

When I was unjustifiably detained by the police twice! I'll admit I was highly offended but I shouldn't have responded based upon how offended I was, I should have responded based upon my intelligence.

Abraham Lincoln said, *"We should be too big to take offense and too noble to give it."*

I realize things are much easier said than done, and telling someone not to become contentious over being offended doesn't make it easy to do. But in order to keep conflict at a minimum and save yourself heartache down the road you have to try and thicken your skin a little bit more. I'm not saying you should allow yourself to be dumped on, I'm saying you need to know when and how to withdraw from a potentially lethal situation. Once again, it doesn't make the other person right or justified in their actions. When it's all said and done it's about your survival and betterment. I don't want to sound "preachy" but I do want to get the message across that we can't change other people's behavior and their initial perception of us, but we can change ourselves and the way we respond to adversity. Granted, in certain situations it doesn't matter what you do or don't do you can't prevent conflict, because the other person is bound and determined to disrupt your life. Even in those instances you still have to keep a level head and not make rash choices in the heat of the moment.

I spoke about developing a thicker skin in order to avoid certain run-ins. As we know, people have no problem with resorting to violence when they feel offended—it happens all the time. We've all seen altercations and brawls whether on TV or right in our own neighborhoods. When someone asks what started the argument, nine times out of ten, you can count on hearing somebody say something like; *he came in here disrespecting my house or my family or me,* or something along those lines. Feeling disrespected is a major cause of contention. So, before reacting adversely, try to do a quick assessment of what's really going on. It won't hurt to take the time to ask yourself if the other person's true intention is to disrespect and offend you or are you taking what's been said or done and attaching your own meaning to it? We have our own built-in mechanism for interpretation whereby we decide within ourselves if a person's intent is to offend, demean or disrespect us. This is another example of how our own perception becomes our reality. Every conflict situation is different, so there's no one-size-fits-all when it comes to dealing with con-frontational encounters. Sometimes the other person has instantly sized you up and tossed you into a negative ste-reotypical category without knowing anything else about you other than how you look. In those instances, their in-tent may very well be to demean and belittle you. But as tough as it is, you have to do your best to stay cool, calm and even-tempered because the other person [or people] has already decided you're guilty until proven innocent; you're incapable until proven capable; you're unqualified until you're proven qualified. So, by all means, try and be the bigger person and take the high road, if at all possible.

By the same token, there are certain situations where there's no malicious intent even though it seems like there is. Society is filled with people who have seriously poor social and people skills. Most, if not all, of them are clueless about how to effectively interact with other people. Sometimes their language is clumsy and easily misinterpreted. Then you're stuck trying to figure out if they meant to offend you personally or if they just say things the wrong way because they're not sharp enough or tactful enough to say them the right way. Case in point: Years ago there was an elderly white woman describing some shoplifters to a mall security guard. In her description of the teenagers she uttered the phrase, "It's hard to say, they all look alike these days." There were a couple of African American women standing nearby and one of them cursed at the old lady and got pretty belligerent with her for making that statement about black people. The security guard intervened and finally quieted the black woman down while the elderly lady stood there perplexed. During all the commotion it was revealed that the shoplifters were three white teenage girls, and the old lady was simply saying most teenage girls look alike to her. So you see, the black woman became instantly offended because she perceived the statement to mean something it didn't. The elderly lady was merely making a general statement about teenagers; how they dress, how they wear their hair, etc., but because of the black woman's perception of what was being said, a big unnecessary ruckus ensued.

Before you allow yourself to feel disrespected and become offended, remember that everyone is different, regardless of what position they hold. Some people are very personable and eloquent when they relate to others. And then there are those people who would have trouble even *spelling* the word etiquette let alone practicing it. Try to assess every situation on a case-by-case basis rather than blanketing everything as an assault because of your race, your age, your size or any other personal characteristic you think might have caused the conflict. It's important to realize that not everything is meant as a personal attack on you; sometimes it's simply the other person's inability to be tactful.

If we're honest with ourselves, I'm sure many of us will admit that to some degree and at one point or another we have allowed ourselves to perpetuate the stereotypical behavior assigned to us by society. I'm speaking specifically about minorities at the moment, but this certainly applies to any group of people. When was the last time someone pushed your buttons and you blew your top in a manner that's generally out of character for you? More often than not, you later regret blowing up like that even though at the time you felt justified. Anger, indignation, feeling disrespected, belittled, put down or demeaned is blinding when it comes to your ability to make a wise choice. I want to reiterate the need to step back, think about YOUR actions and the consequences you could suffer in the future as a result of those actions. Quickly ask yourself, is it worth it?

16

CLOSING THOUGHTS AND REFLECTIONS

We see the world, not as it is, but as we are,

or as we are conditioned to see it.

-Stephen Covey-

This book was not written to shine a light on racial discrimination and profiling. One of my main objectives in writing this book was to stress the importance of learning how to appropriately address conflict and adversity. Another thing I've tried to convey is the importance of understanding the broad spectrum of perception—especially negative perception.

It's easy to get caught up in statistics and allow them to determine the trajectory of your life. Down through the years we've heard the percentages and the data that leads many to believe that if you live in the inner-city you're more prone to crime and less capable of success in life. Nothing could be farther from the truth. It comes down to what you want out of life and how hard you're willing to work for it. If you buy in to the prevailing societal view that you can't be successful because of the neighborhood you live in, or because of your skin color, or because you don't look like someone who can accomplish great things, you've done yourself a terrible injustice if you accept failure as your lot in life. Deep down, I don't believe anyone truly wants to fail. I think it's a defeatist mindset that keeps people from dreaming bigger and pursuing higher goals. If you pour yourself into the mold that others have carved out for you, you're essentially cooperating with your adversary. Living "down" to what society expects of you will leave you with no idea who you really are and what you can accomplish in life. If you live your life acting like you're expected to act and being what you're expected to be you'll end up missing out on what you could have been, because you don't really know who you are until you know who you're not. Every minority group has had to deal with some kind of stereotyping and, unfortunately, that will never change. That's why it's incumbent upon the individual to rise above it.

All of us, at one time or another, will be faced with situations where perceptions will come into play. Taking that into consideration, we have to be mindful of everything we do and how it will be perceived. Sometimes we have to swallow our pride and do or say things we may not want to in an attempt to avoid creating the wrong perception. Taking whatever steps are necessary to avoid negative perceptions won't change who you are as a person, it actually shows that you are in tune with the reality of how the world works. It's very difficult to change someone's perception of you and no matter what you do or say, the perception of you, to some, will never change. But let's not worry about those individuals let's just concentrate on creating the most positive perception of ourselves that we can. It may not always be right but perception is reality.

***

I don't want to deviate too far away from the focal point of the book, but I do want to talk a little bit more about the importance of education and family in this closing chapter. As I mentioned earlier, we can't get disheartened and sidetracked by statistics because it's easy to become just another one. What I mean by that is don't become discouraged when you hear that our educational system in inner cities and other underrepresented communities is failing. It's true that poorly educated students can become somewhat disconnected from the whole academic arena. It's also true that many school districts are seriously underfunded—especially in urban and inner-city areas. But it's also true that students who want to learn <u>are</u> learning and moving forward. In 2013, nine out of ten seniors in San Antonio's largest inner city school district were slated to graduate from high school last year. In addition to that, the dropout rate for that same year fell to around ten percent. Think about it! If ten percent of students in the inner city dropped out, that means ninety-percent didn't!

Statisticians like to paint a grim picture and see the glass as half empty instead of half full. You don't have to become just another statistic simply because word on the street is that schools are failing and therefore you shouldn't bother with committing yourself to education. That's just not true. Don't accentuate the negative. Education is still paramount in your pursuit of success. It doesn't matter what the bleak forecast is for minority education, you can still be a success story. I tell kids it pays to stay in school and it does. Remember, however, you have to step up and take part in your own academic development and progress. It's important to physically attend school, but it's equally important to be there mentally. If you're just occupying a seat and not really interested in absorbing the material, you're only cheating yourself out of what could be a very bright and prosperous future. You have to put something into it to get something out of it.

Pursuing post high school education is not only the key to your financial success, it's also personally fulfilling because it gives you a sense of accomplishment and lets others know that you are an ambitious, success-minded individual. The value of education cannot be over-stated. It isn't a new concept, it's always been a major factor in living a successful life. Unfortunately, I don't think we spend enough time pushing and reiterating it to our young people. We need to emphasize the importance of academic achievement and do everything we can to ignite a passion and yearning for learning in our kids today because when our kids excel and succeed, we all win.

There were several speed bumps throughout my academic career but I didn't allow them to become roadblocks because I realized early on that education was the brush that could paint whatever I wanted on the canvas of my life.

I want to spend a little time talking about the importance of the family unit before I bring this book to a close. As children, home is the first place we develop a sense of belonging. I realize that in these ever-changing times, not every child is growing up in a traditional two-parent home. This trend is not exclusive in minority communities only, it touches every culture. Not everyone is raised in an ivy-covered cottage with a little white picket fence and a dog named Spot.

Even though there are very few families like the "Cleavers" nowadays, there's still a such thing as a family unit. Some kids are raised by grandparents, foster parents, step-parents, others by aunts, uncles, etc. Life happens. And sometimes, there's little you can do when family life situations happen. We have to play the hand we're dealt. Kids in minority inner-city communities are often faced with social and economic issues that don't necessarily affect mainstream suburban communities. We don't live in a bubble or in denial. We see what goes on in minority communities and the problems they face. Many children are being raised in single parent homes where, out of necessity, they're left on their own for long stretches of time. For some, this is an enticement to get involved in reckless behavior. But for others, it prompts them to want something better for themselves and for their children in the years to come. So we have to avoid the tendency to assume that every child raised in a non-traditional family in the inner-city is destined to live a less-than-successful life. We shouldn't paint with such a broad brush all the time because there are many families that are resilient and have overcome the obstacles they faced in their environment. Let's not discount the fact that there are parents in substandard socioeconomic communities who are raising their children to be competent, productive members of society who do not resort to violence or participate in any type of criminal activity.

In this day and age, families aren't only comprised of people who look like you. Parents of all shades, colors, shapes and sizes adopt black kids, white kids, Asian kids, Hispanic kids, kids with physical challenges and other special needs more often than we realize. And those kids grow up to be productive, contributing members of society. But we don't hear about all those success stories, we hear more about the casualties, the breakdown, failure and plight of the inner-city youth because good news doesn't sell too well. There should be less focus on color and more focus on giving a child the love, attention and support they need to live a well-rounded life. I don't think a kid growing up in a non-traditional household without both biological parents is the crux of the problem. I think the main problem is kids growing up without a strong support system of any kind. Maya Angelou said, *when you learn, teach, when you get, give, and try to be a rainbow in someone's cloud.*

Our kids need role models within their family units and also outside their family units. When they see success stories of people who look like them and who faced the same obstacles they face, in some cases worse obstacles than theirs, it encourages them and lets them know they can do it too. Yes, there are some not so encouraging stories and statistics coming out of the inner-city minority communities. However, we can't continue to spotlight and feed on the negatives because if we do, that's all kids will ever see. Their potential will be shrouded by self-doubt and a feeling that they're incapable of being successful in life because of where they come from and how they look. When a person has been made to feel that they're inept or incapable, they're reluctant to even try to accomplish anything. That's a sentiment that crosses all social, economic and racial lines.

I've met many notable people over the years, both professionally and in my personal life. I've even had the privilege of working with doctors who were Nobel Prize winners, quite an honor for someone who just a few years earlier didn't look like he belonged on the campus of a university medical school. I've been successful academically and professionally, but my greatest accomplishment is being the proud father of three wonderful children who not only excel academically but are good kids. They are respectful and considerate of others, and have never had even minor behavioral problems at school. To think I played a part in teaching them how the world works, how to navigate through life and what things are important in life is by far my biggest accomplishment. Without the love and support of my family, I wouldn't be where I am today.

Family indeed plays a key role in the success of an individual. But remember, family doesn't always consist of someone with your DNA. One of the definitions in the dictionary for the word family states in part: *A group of persons who form a household under one head; a basic social unit.* When you're surrounded by people who genuinely love you, support you and want the best for you, you're surrounded by family.

Don't think you can't succeed because you were raised in a single-parent home or a foster home or you didn't have good examples and role models to follow. Don't be afraid to want more out of life than maybe some of your friends want. They might criticize you for not following the crowd. They might try and make you feel like you'll lose your cultural connection and attachment if you step outside your ethnic box and reach for loftier goals. But you don't lose your own personal identity because you want something better out of life.

You belong anyplace you've worked hard to get. If being an athlete or rapper is your heart's desire and what you've aspired to, fine! Great! There's nothing wrong with that. I'm just saying don't take that route because that's all you think you can or should be. I worked hard, I had a goal, and I wasn't going to let anyone or anything stop me. I earned the right to be here.

President Obama once stated, "Change will not come if we wait for some other person or some other time. We are the ones we've been waiting for. We are the change that we seek."

If things are going to change in our minority communities and in society at large, the change has to start with us. We need to be accountable for our actions and set good examples for our children. Just because someone has a negative perception of us and acts upon that opinion, it doesn't mean we have to respond in an explosive manner. If we're ever going to find any kind of common-ground as a nation, the change has to begin with the person in your mirror. Discrimination does exist; it's very real and a part of our everyday lives. But we shouldn't always assume that everything bad that happens is racially motivated or has any other kind of discriminatory connotation. In the long run, it does more harm than good when we rush to judgment or make snappy assumptions about other people's motives. I was a bonafide object of racial profiling but, even so, I still don't believe that every adversarial encounter whether with police or anyone else is racially motivated. Yes, the world can be cold and people can be intentionally cruel sometimes. But sometimes things just happen the way they happen and it has nothing to do with race, class, income bracket, physical/mental status or anything else. It's just life happening. So, we should try our best to assess every situation objectively and avoid reacting the way others expect us to.

I've talked about people who didn't look like they were supposed to be where they ended up and, hopefully, I've reinforced the fact that you belong at any level of success and in any career you desire. Don't become a stumbling block to yourself by thinking you have too many strikes against you to reach a particular goal. There are people who have gone back to finish their education late in life because it was something they always wanted to do. There was an article a year or so ago about an 85-year-old woman who said she always regretted not finishing college, so she went back to school at age eighty-five to get her degree… and she did! It's all about determination and refusing to throw in the towel just because someone else may think you don't look right in a certain role. Whatever your life situation is, it's only a hindrance if you allow it to be.

On a side note, it's also important to keep in mind that you shouldn't expect special treatment simply because you're a minority or you have some other life-challenge. To expect any kind of special treatment would suggest you don't believe you're as capable as others to work hard and succeed on your own ability. I stated in an earlier chapter that sometimes we can have a negative perception of ourselves. Most often it's in the form of low self-esteem and a poor self-image. Those negative "self-perceptions" can, in some instances, be just as toxic and detrimental as the ones we face from other people. If you don't realize your full potential because it's shrouded in a poor self-image and low self-esteem, you run the risk of torpedoing all the things you could accomplish in life if you only had a stronger belief in your ability. Many people lash out in anger because of how they feel about themselves. We're our own worst critics sometimes. But when we feel better about ourselves we feel better about the world around us.

From a very young age we start to develop a sense of who we are, how we look, what we like about ourselves and what we don't like about ourselves. Much of the opinion we develop about ourselves is based upon how others feel and interact with us. If someone else's negative perception of you starts to make you feel that maybe you don't belong at a higher level or in a certain place, remember their opinion of you is totally invalid and you shouldn't allow it to alter your self-image. If you keep pressing on, working hard and holding your head up through whatever adversity you might face, eventually, people will see that their negative perception of you was wrong!

Regardless of what anyone says or how others have made you feel, everyone has equal value no matter who they are.

Whether you're considered a minority or the majority, we all have things we've had to deal with on a social level. Everyone has been faced with some kind of societal woe. As time passes, some obstacles become bigger, while others get smaller but, nevertheless, we'll still face some kind of challenge as we go through life. Our kids are struggling to fit in, grappling for acceptance and trying to find their identity and place in a world that has forever changed. The kids of this present generation face far more difficulties than their parents did. And because of that, it's of paramount importance that kids have good examples and role models to follow as they navigate through the troubled waters of present day society. That's why speaking, at schools in particular, is such a passion of mine. I want kids to know they don't have to succumb to the notion that success isn't for them simply because of how they look or what side of the tracks they were born on.

Even if you had a less than ideal start in life; even if no one else seems to be rooting for you or believing in you, you can still believe in yourself. When you're working hard and doing what it takes to fulfill your dreams and reach your goals, if some naysayer comes along and tells you, "You don't look like you're supposed to be here," remember it doesn't matter how you look or what challenges you face, you can hold your head high, square your shoulders and say with confidence, "I *AM* supposed to be here!

DR. DONALD ARNETTE
AUTHOR. SPEAKER. COACH.

If you or your organization are planning an event and want your audience to be inspired, motivated, armed with the skills necessary to resolve adversity and be in a position to get the most out of life experiences, book Dr. Arnette at your next event.

Instagram: @docarnette
Twitter: @docarnette
Facebook: @Dr. donald Arnette
For booking information: booking@docarnette.com